SYMBOLS OF
FREEMASONRY

Assouline Publishing
601 West 26th Street,
New York, NY 10001
www.assouline.com

© 2000 Assouline Publishing for the present edition
First published in French by Editions Assouline
Les Symboles des Francs-Maçons © 1997 Editions Assouline

Distributed in all countries, excluding France,
Belgium, Luxemburg, USA and Canada,
by Thames and Hudson Ltd (Distributors), London

ISBN: 2 84323 201 5

Translated by Ian Monk

Printed in Italy

SYMBOLS OF
FREEMASONRY

DANIEL BÉRESNIAK
PHOTOGRAPHS BY LAZIZ HAMANI

EDITIONS ASSOULINE

CONTENTS

PREFACE

Freemasons prosper in all free countries and wherever there is law and order. They are victimised and persecuted in all states governed by the whims of an autocratic ruler or a single party, and in places where all truth is considered to be found in a single book which is raised on a pedestal, a fixed monument.

In the city, that teeming mass of isolated people inhabiting today's urban sprawls, the Masonic lodge is a place where people can come together in a spirit of fraternal joy. The Rule, rites and symbols, allow every person to become themselves: to discover that they are all makers of meaning; to recognise themselves and others as sources of light adding to the general light, while accepting that no one of these single flames can shed light everywhere. Masonic teaching is known as "The Royal Art", a term which used to be applied to alchemy. Many books exist on this subject, but they are generally so strange and difficult to understand as to infuriate any reader who is unused to going beyond the literal meaning of things. However, there are two aspects of the Royal Art—the tradition from which Freemasons draw most of their symbols—which should encourage us to examine it more closely. The first reveals its central role in the history of human behaviour. Whenever an all-embracing orthodoxy has the power to exclude or kill those who have doubts or ask questions,

whenever the pressure to conform is so heavily imposed that dissenters are threatened with death, free spirits have always found the means of sharing and spreading their ideas. This may involve veiling them in allegory or wrapping them up in thick layers of lies and absurdity.

The second aspect, which leads on from the first, places the Royal Art firmly within the history of ideas. Even today, all the metaphors which allude to the act of becoming, and which we still now use to describe reality, derive from the vocabulary of alchemy. The act of becoming is a metamorphosis. This concept underscores Masonic thought.

A metamorphosis takes place during a journey through different landscapes, among forms and colours, during which each of us is transformed. But, in this context, the term has intentionally been trivialised into the act of putting on a costume and playing a role. Those who undertake this adventure come out of it with varying rewards, depending on the landscape they visit, their approach, what they make of it and how much of it they see. A journey of initiation is not a package tour. There are no sign-posts. The risk of becoming lost, of sliding back when attempting to go forwards, is what gives life to the unexpected. The intertwining of danger and promise creates the possibility of understanding and allows the idea of freedom to be considered a moral value. What Freemasons have to offer is the notion of a society created around the union of diversity; the opposite of a union of conformity.

This book is a collection of the symbolic images which Freemasons encounter on their journeys of transformation.[1] The texts and illustrations form an intimate dialogue whose subject is Freemasonry, and which casts light on the relationship between dreams and reality, reason, intuition and imagination. Anyone who delves into the history of ideas must ask themselves questions about the connections between current ideologies and traditional, timeless representations of the world. Such questions inevitably lead to a study of the symbols of Freemasonry, to watching Freemasons live with these symbols and myths, and to listening to them debate the subject. They are delighted not to all have the same opinions, for debate is vital to a culture. Freemasonry is indeed a culture and, like all cultures, is a living fire where answers fuel new questions.

The way in which Freemasonry uses symbolism gives us an insight into the word itself. Masonic symbolism is based on the notion of building: building, becoming and making. "To make" is understood as "to make something of oneself". This approach forges a relationship between the physical roads we walk along in the city on our way home and the spiritual paths which in each of us lead between our desires and our thoughts.

Freemasons delve into myths in order to understand how the human mind works, with a view to becoming free people, which is to say, people who act rather than react. During their journeys, they cast aside their layman's rags in order to don their costume of light and live out different roles. In this way Freemasons are able to experience a reality which is often denied to or simply ignored by those people bound by the prejudices and certitudes of current, fashionable philosophies. Imagination and reason feed off each other even, and perhaps especially, when they are opposed.

Freemasonry's symbols are a part of our culture and of our lives, in the spiritual, intellectual and ethical realms as well as in our ordinary daily routines.

1. Editor's note: This work is a translation of a text written by a French Mason. Some of the content is peculiar to France and will not be known to other Masons. Nevertheless, the basic principles described and explained are common to Freemasonry wherever it is practiced throughout the world.

INTRODUCTION

I. THE MASON'S PATH
AND THE FUNCTION OF SYMBOLS

Symbolism looks at the world as if it were a text. It involves thinking about thought and speaking about language. As its etymology suggests, a symbol is an image made up of various elements in such a way that the whole represents more than the sum of its parts.

The first degree initiation ritual, that of Entered Apprentice, states: "Here, all is symbol." This statement describes the path to follow: "Here, we learn to look at the symbolic nature of everything that exists." In other words, everything should be seen as a metaphor. This point must be stressed, because symbolism is so often looked upon as merely a codified language, recognisable to members of the same group and nothing more.

In fact, the use of symbolism destroys fossilised definitions which no longer fit a changing reality. It causes us to accept the transitory nature of being, constantly in the process of becoming something else. The point is to recognise reality's true, living nature, to recognise the porousness of the boundaries that separate categories, in other words to "gather what is scattered".

Of course, symbolism can free us from preconceptions and knee-jerk reactions, only in so far as it is not dogmatic. If it becomes merely a set of memorised responses to a litany of simplistic equations, such as "this means that", then our spirits will become diminished and alienated instead of being enriched. The same remedy can either kill or cure us. The difference is a matter of quantity: it depends on the dosage and the situation. Symbolism opens the doors of perception when it explores the links between desires and ideas, imagination and reason, the mind which generalises and the mind which dissects, but only if it guarantees both elements their share and doesn't lose itself in comfortable prejudices.

Working with symbolism can have a practical application when it helps us undermine our automatic responses and link words to their origin. It corrects the formation of prejudices which in turn generate aberrant behaviour. Symbolism is immune from the drift towards the occult which often accompanies esoteric study. It does not confuse devotion with mysticism, faith with trust or servility with good will. It teaches us to think clearly and behave better.

The Masons' viewpoint can be defined by two ideas which are repeated again and again during all the Masonic rites: "to reach further" and "to gather what is scattered". It is by responding to these exhortations that progress is made towards objective knowledge. For the mental processes which are needed to develop these theories and their practical applications involve acts of synthesis, association and application. It is these which are vital for the completion of the Mason's project.

The square and compasses are indissolubly linked. They indicate the interaction between mind and matter and stand for the progression from the material to the spiritual.

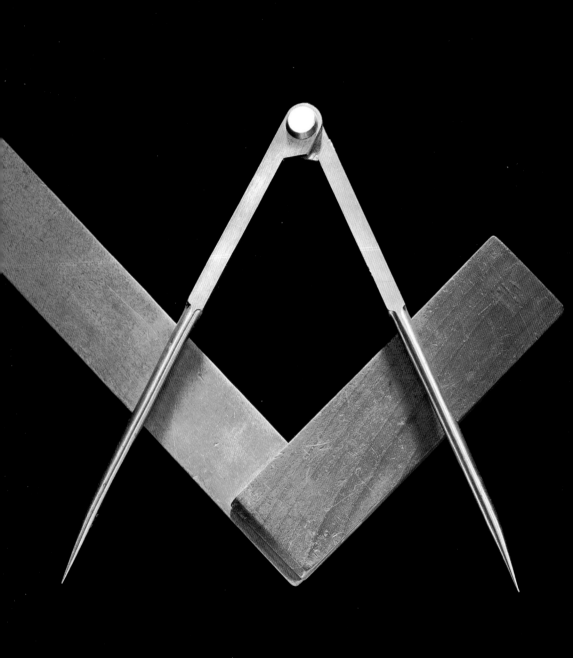

Symbolism emphasises subjective knowledge. The use of symbolism encourages a form of introspection through free association, linking individual and collective history, as well as the laws governing all things. Symbolists postulate that objective knowledge can only be approached through subjective knowledge, as in the Socratic aphorism, "Know thyself and thou shalt know the world and the gods". Recognising this, Masons explore the relationship between desires and ideas and pick apart all dogmatic statements, even such dogmas as are based on proof. They explore the different layers of meaning, performing the task urged upon us by Spinoza, when he said, "You say that you have chosen an idea because it is right. Know that you believe it is right precisely because you have chosen it." Jacob ben Sheshet, a cabbalist of the Gerona School, invited us to perform a similar experiment: "When you say 'God created man in his image' and when you say 'Man created God in his image', you believe that you are saying the opposite and, in a literal (*pshatt*) sense, that is true. It is up to you to study and meditate until you understand why and how you are saying the same thing in different ways."

Thanks to their familiarity with symbolism, Freemasons recognise the mythological aspect of any discourse. What better proof is there that the use of symbolism gathers what is scattered?

II. RITES AND RITUALS

A rite is a formal act, and a ritual is a set order for the carrying out of rites. Let us look at them first of all in the context of biology. They are actually techniques for increasing the efficiency of communication (or signalling) and serve to create a network of ties between different members of a group. In animals, ritualisation is seen to decrease the use of violence. It exists before language. As for human beings, it enables us to look at ourselves from the outside and view ourselves as objects of study. To a biologist, therefore, rites and rituals perform a vital function. From an anthropological point of view, they are seen to become more and more diversified and complicated, as they evolve from the simple to the complex.

Freemasons are interested in rites because they want to understand how human beings and society operate, with a view to "preparing the coming of a better and more enlightened society". This sentence is an extract from a Masonic ritual. Masons explore how rites function and how traditional and religious rites are observed in every nation, according to specific social codes and life-styles. All Masons are asked to contribute to the study of this subject.

Masonic rituals set down the order of rites and the way in which they are carried out. There are many of them and they have evolved over time. As for the rites themselves, they are extremely similar and any Mason who travels may come in for a surprise, but will never feel completely lost. The degrees—Entered Apprentice, Fellow and Master—are the same in every rite. Entered Apprentices are always initiated after three symbolic journeys, during which they must confront the elements of earth, water, air and fire. Fellows undertake five journeys, at the end of which they contemplate the Blazing Star. As for the Masters, they must relive the passion of Hiram, the murdered architect.

In all the rituals observed throughout the world Entered Apprentices, Fellows and Masters work in lodges, symbolic representations of Solomon's Temple with its two pillars, Jachin and Boaz. The temple lies on the east-west axis. To the east sits the Master in the Chair, or Worshipful Master, who presides over the assembly. To the west sits the Tyler or Inner Guard who watches over the threshold. To the north sit the Entered Apprentices who are required to remain silent. To the south sit the Fellows. Masters may sit wherever they choose. The Entered Apprentices and Fellows work respectively under the direction of the Junior and Senior Wardens. Everywhere, work begins "at noon" and stops "at the stroke of midnight". These times are, of course, symbolic and serve as a reminder that in this place and during this period of time each person must step away from their daily existence and make the effort of experiencing a moment outside of time. In every lodge the vault of the ceiling is decorated with stars, to show that the temple acts as a mediator between human beings and the universe. Everyone enters wearing an apron and gloves, and works symbolically with the tools of a Mason: square, compasses, gauge, lever, plumb rule, plumb line and trowel.

Last but not least, the brother (or the sister) who speaks addresses the Master in the Chair and standing "to attention" must not be interrupted until they close their speech with the words "I have spoken".

Evidence of the great diversity of rites is to be seen in the different ways in which the temples are laid out, in the texts of the rituals which describe the initiation ceremonies and the running of meetings, as well as in the regulations for appointing officers of the lodge. But the major difference lies in the degrees of advancement after that of Master. The two pillars, Jachin and Boaz, which stand at either side of the temple door are positioned differently depending on whether the Ancient and Accepted Scottish Rite or the French Rite is being practiced. In Emulation Working, each of the Wardens has a small column on their table, which one Warden lowers when the other raises theirs. In the Rectified Scottish Rite, a broken column bearing the inscription *adhuc stat* (in Latin, it is still standing) is positioned inside the temple. In Emulation Working, officers are appointed by means of a yearly rota, while in the other rites these officers (the Worshipful Master, the two Wardens, the Secretary, the Treasurer, the Orator, the Almoner, the Master of Ceremonies and the Tyler or Inner Guard) may all be elected. Sometimes the Worshipful Master may be elected and then allowed to choose officers, or else the Worshipful Master is appointed by a committee. Co- and female Masonry practice the same rites as male Masonry, although some male lodges do not accept any "sisters" and some female ones do not accept any "brothers".

The main difference between the rites lies in the degrees of advancement, or "High Grades". There are seven of them in the French Rite, six in the Rectified Scottish Rite, thirty-three in the Ancient and Accepted Scottish Rite, and between ninety and ninety-nine in the rites of Memphis, Mizraïm and Memphis-Mizraïm. Protocols between the rites in France have established a system of equivalences in order to enable Freemasons to visit lodges which practice a different rite from their own. Readers wishing to learn more about this subject have many books at their disposal. Although Freemasons work in lodges that are said to be "duly tiled", that is to say isolated from other people and from exterior disturbances, Freemasonry is not a secret society, but one manifestation of cultural and social life. The outside world influences it and is in turn influenced by it. It reflects and radiates.

One final important fact needs to be made clear: Freemasonry is not a religion. Yet, each ceremony ends, in the manner of religious ceremonies, with a collection in which everyone is asked to give alms for charitable purposes. Freemasons call the almsbox the "broken column".

Since the eighteenth century, Masonic lodges have grouped together in federations. These federations make up what is termed "modern Freemasonry".

The most important text of modern Freemasonry was compiled by various authors and is entitled *The Constitutions of the Freemasons*. It was published anonymously in 1723, but is always associated with James Anderson

(1684–1739), a pastor in the Scottish Presbyterian Church. He was commissioned to edit it and his work was then submitted to a committee of fourteen "learned" brethren, who approved it after making some corrections and changes. This text was intended to be read out in the lodges each time a new member joined.

The first article of the *Constitutions* states that people must be judged according to their conduct, and not their religious opinion:

"A *Mason* is oblig'd, by his Tenure,[1] to obey the moral Law; and if he rightly understands the Art, he will never be a stupid **Atheist**, nor an irreligious **Libertine**. But though in ancient Times Masons were charg'd in every Country to be of the Religion of that Country or Nation, whatever it was, yet 'tis now thought more expedient only to oblige them to that Religion in which all Men agree, leaving their particular Opinions to themselves; that is, to be *good Men and true*, or Men of Honour and Honesty, by whatever Denominations or Persuasions they may be distinguish'd; whereby Masonry becomes the *Center of Union*, and the Means of conciliating true Friendship among Persons that must have remain'd at a perpetual Distance."

The idea that a person may be worthy of respect, no matter what their religion, falls within an ancient tradition of tolerance and open-mindedness, but it ran against the dominant ideology of the beginning of the eighteenth century. After about one and a half centuries of Religious Wars, a fragile peace had been estab-

A tracing board showing the first apartment of the Rose-Croix grade (Ancient and Accepted Scottish rite). Lodge of Mons (Belgium), eighteenth century.

SAGESSE

FOY

ORIENT

FORCE

SEPTENTRION

MIDI

CHARITÉ

BEAUTEZ

L'OCCIDENT

FORCE

lished based on the division of nations between the opposing currents of Christianity. According to the principle of *cuius regio, cuius religio* everyone had to accept the religion of their ruler.

At the time of Anderson's *Constitutions*, England and France were prey to intolerance and fanaticism. In England, Catholics were persecuted; in France it was the Protestants. The English Civil War had been a Protestant revolution which had led to the deposition and death of the Catholic King Charles I. After the death of Cromwell, the royal family reinstated itself with Charles II, who professed to being Anglican, but the Protestant Parliament greatly feared that Catholicism would regain power under James II. In 1688 he was deposed and before declaring William of Orange and his wife Mary joint sovereigns, Parliament insisted on them adopting the Bill of Rights which stopped anyone who was Catholic, or married to a Catholic, from ascending to the throne. During this difficult period, Catholics, who were pejoratively called papists, were not allowed to live in London, their taxes were doubled and they were not permitted to own a weapon or a horse of any value. They also lost the right to buy or inherit land. In 1713, after the death of William, Queen Mary strengthened the old 1605 Test Act and the following year took away the Catholics' right to teach.

In France, after the repeal of the Edict of Nantes in 1685, Protestants no longer had the right to practice their religion. After the declaration of 1724, all religious gatherings except Catholic ones were forbidden. Protestants and those who supported them risked the death penalty and only Catholics could hold public office.

At this time, intolerance was a guiding principle: birth and religion were seen as reliable ways of judging people. Both the persecutors and the persecuted, the dominators and the dominated, were convinced that they belonged to a group of chosen people who were up against the Devil's minions. Only by despising others could they maintain their self-esteem. The persecutors were more than just the enemies of the persecuted, they offered a role model to be emulated. Cruelty—the manifestation of power and of the pleasure of wielding power—became fully self-justified in this fanatical obsession with purity and faith!

Talk of the pure and the impure, the chosen and the damned, or the struggle between light and darkness, are examples of the ways in which thought can be made the lackey of automatic responses, and ideology be made to support gut instinct. Above all, such divisions deny the truth that reality is grey, contradictory and paradoxical; that Life evolves, diversifies and becomes more complex thanks to these contradictions and to those forces which generate energy precisely because they are opposed.

People have always known this and have been saying it for ever. Generation after generation they have affirmed the absolute superiority of the individual over the group. They have argued that it is impossible to reduce identity to membership of a group and they have valiantly defended the freedom of opinion.

Sixty years before Anderson's *Constitutions* for example, in 1662, the Royal Society for the Protection of Natural Knowledge was founded. Jean Théophile Desaguliers (1683–1739), co-author of the Masonic *Constitutions* and, in 1719, Grand Master of the Lodge of England, was one of its most active members. The Royal Society's founding Charter was to be an inspiration to the authors of the 1723 *Constitutions* who said of it: "As for the members who make up the ranks of the Society, let it be noted that they include people of a variety of different religions, countries and ways of thinking. The Society saw itself obliged to extend its franchise in this way in order to fulfil the breadth of its own declared ambitions.

"They openly profess to want to lay the foundations not for an English, Scottish, Irish, Papist or Protestant philosophy, but for a philosophy which encompasses the whole of human kind. By gathering together men of all countries they are creating a favourable basis for the future continuous exchange of ideas between all nations, which will make the Royal Society the central bank and repository of world knowledge."

In passing, it must be stressed that love of knowledge has always been associated with a love of life. Those who continue to learn free themselves from old-fashioned responses and come to respect humanity in general. Those who claim that a person's birth is a mark of their quality are either ignorant, or else are taking advantage of other people's ignorance. Thirty years before the Royal Society was founded, Galileo

had been tried (February 1633). Thirty years before that, Giordano Bruno had been burned at the stake in Rome. Between those two dates, Vanino Vanini had been burned alive at the age of thirty-five for having dared to mock religion and its dogmas (1619). Like endless echoes of Socrates' trial, voices have been raised in argument and counter-argument. There are those who want to stop history, freezing it into an eternal present defined by an unchanging revealed truth, and those who recognise movement and take pleasure in searching out and defining a truth which is constantly changing.

The partisans of an already defined truth impose their dogmas by force, in order to enjoy the power of ruling others. They speak of love and yet they kill in its name, promoting the ideal of a golden tomorrow. Such truths may be religious, political, philosophic or even scientific. But they are always monolithic, all-embracing and totalitarian, maintained by a chorus of official voices, be they clergymen, mandarins or *apparatchiks*. Submission is all that is required from their voluntary or enforced followers, who may be collectively termed the "faithful" or even "militants".

This dogmatic way of thinking comes from a denial of reality as ever-changing, and thus can be considered to be pathological. But every poison has its antidote and other voices rise up in answer, to remind us of the promise as well as the dangers of reality.

Looking back through history, we come across the Rosicrucians, Comenius, Francis Bacon and Tommaso Campanella. In Florence, we meet an ancient Greek called Plethon, whom Marsilio Ficino described as being "almost a second Plato". This man was involved in setting-up Florence's Platonic Academy which, two centuries before the Royal Society, brought together men of intelligence and learning, artists, poets, doctors, astronomers and those learned in the ancient tongues, to discuss mankind and the city, and to discuss major issues from an interdisciplinary point of view. Plethon spoke the following words in public: "Each religion, my brethren, is but a shard of Aphrodite's broken mirror."[2]

This tradition of tolerance and open-mindedness can be traced back even further. It is epitomised by true mystics, that is to say by men who remain open to self doubt and self-criticism. In the Christian world they are exemplified by the Rhineland mystics, in the Muslim world by the Sufis and in the Jewish world by the cabbalists. All of these mystics were disliked by the establishment and by the clergy—be it Christian, Islamic or Jewish—which claimed to represent them. For institutions require devoted followers not mystical seers, because what they seek is power, not truth. This is why the creation of an institution marks the death of truth. In the same tradition are the Biblical prophets who spoke out against their kings and high priests, shattering the certainties of the ordinary people who were sunk into a rut of accepted belief.

It is within this tradition that Freemasonry takes its place and within whose literature the essential Masonic texts exist, from the *Old Charges* to Anderson's *Constitutions*.

III. OPERATIVE FREEMASONRY AND SPECULATIVE FREEMASONRY

Contrary to an old belief, which has been defended by many historians in the past, we are now in a position to demonstrate that Speculative (meaning theoretical or philosophical) Freemasonry did not derive directly from Operative (or working) Freemasonry. In the seventeenth and eighteenth centuries, Freemasons took their inspiration from the rites and customs of the Guild of Masons in order to give their work the structure, organisation and symbols necessary to fulfil a specific purpose. This was to gather together people of different origins and different opinions and enable them to work on a common project: the creation of a temple for the whole of humanity.

Rather than saying that Freemasonry was born out of the Guild of Masons, it might be more helpful to say that learned men who wished to work together and exchange ideas adopted the symbolism and structures used by working masons.

For indeed, the symbolism of the Mason's tools does enable a variety of different kinds of knowledge to be linked.

1. In Feudal Law this meant "the act or fact of holding a tenement". By extension it here means a person's rights and duties.
2. D. Béresniak, *Les Premiers Médicis et l'Académie platonicienne de Florence*. Détrad, Paris, 1985.

Crossed square and compasses surrounding the letter "G", for geometry.

CHAPTER 1

THE CALENDAR

DATING THE CREATION OF THE UNIVERSE

THE TEMPLE IS AN IMAGE OF THE WORLD AND THE BEGINNING OF THE WORLD ESTABLISHES TIME. THE MASONIC WORLD IS SYMBOLICALLY coeval with the universe and refers to the moment of creation as the *anno lucis*, Year of Light, or Year of Masonry. English masons took their dates from James Ussher, an Anglican priest born in Dublin in 1580, who published his *Annals of the Old and the New Testaments* in around 1650.

According to Ussher's reading of the Bible, 4,004 B.C. is the date of the Creation. Generally accepted by the various English churches at the start of the eighteenth century, this chronology was also adopted by Anderson's *Constitutions*, the basic text of modern Freemasonry which dates from the same period.

The Masonic date adds four thousand years to the currently accepted origins of the Christian era, or Year of Our Lord. It is less than three centuries off the date given by the Jewish calendar which, in its present form, dates from the fourth century B.C. and counts the years since the creation of the world according to its own reading of the Bible.

The Masonic year generally begins in March, a tradition which is observed particularly in France. For example, April 10, 1996 is "the tenth day of the second month of the year 5996 of Light". In the past, the Hebrew names of the months were used, but this practice has now been abandoned, except in some lodges of the Scottish Rite.

This calendar is not accepted everywhere. The masons of the Ancient and Accepted Scottish Rite, and in particular those at the grade of Knight Kadosh, use the Hebrew months and a calendar based on Jewish chronology, or *anno hebraico*, also known as *anno mundi*. This calender begins in mid-September and adds 3,760 years onto the Gregorian calendar.

At the grade of Royal Arch, the date of Creation is 530 B.C., the date when building was started on the second temple by Zerubbabel. This year is called the *anno inventionis*.

At the degree of Royal and Select Master, which is used mostly in England and in the United States, time begins with the dedication of Solomon's temple, that is to say in 1,000 B.C., known as the *anno depositionnis*.

The templar degrees which derive from the Strict Templar Observance, a rite practiced in the Germanic states in the eighteenth and nineteenth centuries, count from the date of the

This transcript of a Masonic meeting from the year of the French Revolution is dated according to both the Christian and Masonic calendars, 1789 and 5789.

Nous Officiers et Membres de la R∴ L∴
Française S∴ Joseph des Arts regulierement consti[tuée]
aux E∴ R∴ L∴ L∴ Regulieres repandües sur la Surf[ace]
de la Terre : g par le nombre Misterieux, Declarons et
attestons à tous les hommes qui connoissent la vraye
Lumiere ; que le S∴ [...] Francois Vidal natif de foix
a été successivement reçu par nous Aprenti, Compagnon
Maître Maçon ; qu'il [...] Zelle pour nos travaux [...]
[...] le [...] recommandable et Cher
à tous les Frères ; En Foi de quoy nous lui avons d[onné]
present, qu'il a signé avec nous et devant vous et a[...]
le Surprize, nous lui avons fait aposer le Sceau det[...]
de notre Architecture, afin qu'il recoive de tous les Freres
Toye Satisfaction & Bon Acuil ; leur offrant le recipro[que]
en pareil Cas : fait et delivré et Loge regulierement
assemblé ; A L∴ D∴ de Toulouse le 30eme Jour
du Sixieme Mois de l'an de la Vray Lumiere
5789 [...] vulgaire le 30 Aoust
1789 ∴∴

founding of the Order of the Temple in A.D. 1118. This is the *anno ordinis*. Famous German Freemasons, such as Goethe, Lessing, Herder and Wieland, practiced this rite.

During the French Revolution, those French lodges that were still active in 1793 adopted the revolutionary calendar, which was invented by a Freemason, Charles Gilbert Romme (1750–95).

During the course of their symbolic journeys, Freemasons cast aside their layman's clothes and allow historical and legendary characters to dress them in robes of light. At each place they visit, there exists a time, or dimension, of the temple, whose beginning corresponds to a specific project. The Old Testament tradition defines man as a partner of the Creator. The Book of Genesis (*Bereschit* 2,3) states that the Eternal blessed the seventh day and sanctified it because "he rested on the seventh day after all the work he had been doing" (*acher bara Elohim la'asoth*). Later on, the text of Genesis points out that man was created to cultivate the earth and, once created, was "settled ... in the garden of Eden to cultivate and take care of it" (*Bereschit* 2,15).

In the Judæo-Christian culture, Masons accept the Biblical image of a constantly changing creation and define their mission as a continuation of the work started by the Great Architect of the Universe. Given the fact that they see themselves as heirs to a world in the process of being constructed, it is natural that they should place themselves in it from the very beginning of its foundation, which the Jewish calendar represents both allegorically and symbolically. This explains why the most common practice among Masons, from the first degree of Apprenticeship onwards, is to add four thousand years to the Christian date, thus symbolically associating themselves with the Light which was shed on the foundations of a work that is still to be completed.

This very notion of dating the Creation has meaning and provides food for thought only if it is seen as being symbolic, that is to say if it is seen as forging a link between a reality which is still to be determined, and our natural desire to experience that reality as if it were already fully determined.

A nineteenth-century Masonic calendar, based on the lunar calendar, showing lunar months, solar years and the Hebraic months.

CALENDRIER MAÇONNIQUE
POUR LE 19ᵉ SIÈCLE.

MOIS LUNAIRES.	ANNÉES SOLAIRES.	
	1820 *. 1839. 1858. 1877. 1896 *.	1821. 1840 *. 1859. 1878. 1897.
NISAN	16 Mars.	5 Mars.
JIAR	14 Avril.	4 Avril.
SIVAN	14 Mai.	3 Mai.
THAMOUZ. . . .	12 Juin.	2 Juin.
AB.	12 Juillet.	1ᵉʳ Juillet.
ELOUL	10 Août.	31 Juillet.
THISCHRI. . . .	9 Septembre.	29 Août.
MARHESCHVAN.	8 Octobre.	28 Septembre.
CHISLEV	7 Novembre.	27 Octobre.
TEVETH.	6 Décembre.	26 Novembre.
SCHEBAT	5 Janvier.	25 Décembre.
ADAR.	4 Février.	24 Janvier.
VEADAR.		22 Février.
Nombre d'Or.	16.	17.
Cycle hébraïque.	13.	14.

CHAPTER 2

THE CHAMBER OF REFLECTION

PREPARATION FOR A JOURNEY

THE CHAMBER OF REFLECTION, PRESENT ONLY IN CERTAIN MASONIC RITES, IS A SMALL ROOM IN WHICH THE CANDIDATES ARE LEFT ON THEIR own for a period before the initiation ceremony begins.[1] Seated at a table, they write their Philosophical Will, which is later to be read out in the lodge.

Isolation in a hut or cave begins a ritual during which a symbolic metamorphosis is experienced; like a chrysalis hatching out of its cocoon the initiate comes out of the darkness a new person. Such a custom is usual amongst all peoples and in all places where initiation rites are traditional. It serves to separate the neophytes from their family and to make them consider the notions of death and rupture. The Chamber of Reflection is a modern, updated form of the ancient cave of initiation.

The initiate is alone with a sheet of paper and a pencil. The Chamber of Reflection is lit only by a candle which casts its feeble light on a number of ornaments: a human skull, some bones, a lump of bread, a flask of water, an hourglass, a saucer containing salt and another containing sulphur. On the wall, are murals painted in white on a black background: a cockerel, a scythe, and the word VITRIOL or VITROLUM

which is the ancient command to examine oneself—*visita interiora terrae, rectificando invenies occultam lapidem*: (visit the centre of the earth and by rectifying you shall find the hidden stone).

These symbols derive from alchemy, a tradition which has provided us with all of the symbols we use today to describe metamorphosis. Salt, which is extracted from sea water by evaporation, is fire delivered from water. As for sulphur, alchemists believed that it is to the body what the sun is to the earth. The coupling of salt and sulphur is an image of ambivalence, of life and death, of light and darkness nourishing one another. For Masons, the sojourn in the Chamber of Reflection is the "trial and proof of earth". The first lesson to be learnt is that nothing is intrinsically good or bad. Only people, like builders, can make something good or bad, depending on how they use it. We may already understand this idea intellectually, but intellectual knowledge is not enough. Ritual ceremonies, myths and symbols are used to facilitate the shift from knowledge to experience, that is to say, from what has been conceptualised to what has been lived out.

The hourglass is an invitation to reflect on

Before being admitted, candidates are led into the Chamber of Reflection, where they mèditate and write their Philosophical Wills. The notice on the wall warns: "Vitriol. If curiosity brings you here then LEAVE! There is still time."

VIGILANCE
PERSÉVÉRANCE.
V.I.T.R.I.O.L.
Si la curiosité t'amène ici
VA-T-EN !
Il en est temps encore

the reversibility of time; the bread denotes the vital transformation from the raw to the cooked; and water represents fertility. So knowledge has to be reexamined, not to increase its ontological qualities, but to alter them; "not to fill up a vase, but to light a fire", as Montaigne put it. This quotation from the author of the *Essays* leads us to the cockerel, which announces the appearance of light. It is associated with Mercury/Hermes who sets limits and helps us to cross them. The ability to associate things by distinguishing between them is proof of the passage from knowledge to experience.

As for the scythe, the tool used for reaping, it is only since the fifteenth century that it has been put in the hands of a skeleton to represent death, the great leveller. This image confirms and illustrates the teaching revealed in the other symbols: death in the vegetable world is a source of life for the animal world.

These symbols focus the neophytes' attention on the need to recognise reality as it is, and to free themselves from those phantoms which set light and darkness in opposition. This initial trial and proof of earth in the Chamber of Reflection shows the way forward: to replace the word "or", and its resulting attitudes, by the word "and".

For energy is, in fact, the fruit of contradictory forces which resist each other. In the body, energy is called tension. If it is excessive, then it can be lethal. But so can a lack of it. Only between these two extremes is life possible. The Royal Art, which used to be a term for alchemy and is now used in Freemasonry, is precisely that: the art of finding the happy medium.

The exhortation to "gather what is scattered",—which is frequently uttered during Masonic rituals,—reconciles contradictions by seeing them as complementary opposites. We all experience the desire to conform and the desire to be exceptional; the desire to be one thing, then another; to remain and to move on; to believe and to doubt. By replacing "or" by "and" we give contradictions legitimacy as the linchpin between chaos and order, between turbulence and stillness.

Conflicts between people may be seen as the echo of the interior conflicts we all experience. And if reality is to be perceived as shadowy and in the process of changing, from its simplest manifestations to its most complex and diverse, then it can be approached only by words. It is only what we can say about it. Symbolism is a way of showing how words create images and how these images become elements of myths, imaginary tales which have the ring of truth because they run on the winding paths that lead from desires to ideas.

The Chamber of Reflection is the place where the exploration of these paths begins. The bread, salt, hourglass, cockerel and scythe are images which, when they are brought together, raise these vital questions.

1. The Chamber exists in the Ancient and Accepted Scottish rite and Continental European lodges but not in the Emulation rite.

A skull and various alchemical symbols accompany the candidates during the trial and proof of earth.

CHAPTER 3

KING SOLOMON'S TEMPLE

A COMMUNITY OF BROTHERS

IN THE COOKE MANUSCRIPT (1410), ONE OF THE OLDEST KNOWN TEXTS WHICH DEALS WITH FREEMASONRY, WE READ THAT: "AT the time of the construction of the Temple of Solomon, begun by King David ... Solomon employed 24,000 Masons and ... Solomon confirmed the rights which his father David had bestowed upon the Masons. Solomon himself taught them their methods (that is to say their traditions and practices) which are not very different from those of today."

Operative masons who read this text saw it is a historical truth. They believed that they were plying a craft which dated back to the time of King Solomon, and which he had codified.

However, the date of the construction of King Solomon's temple has not always been the key date in the Freemasons' cosmology. This central role was once given to the Tower of Babel. The *Regius* manuscript, which predates *Cooke* by twenty years, cites King Nemrod, the builder of that famous tower, as "the first and most excellent master". He it was, and not King Solomon, who gave the Masons their first "charge", their rules of conduct and professional code.

For a long time both King Solomon and King Nemrod played a part in the tradition. A

Masonic text known as the *Thistle* manuscript, of 1756, says that Nemrod "created the Masons" and "gave them their signs and terms so that they could distinguish themselves from other people ... it was the first time that the Masons were organised as a craft."

It was during the early years of the eighteenth century that Freemasonry stopped seeing its origins in the Tower of Babel and that Solomon alone was considered "the first Grand Master".

The eighteenth-century Masonic texts shed light on the ideas and attitudes at the time of the shift from Operative Masonry to Speculative Masonry. These texts are called the "early catechisms" and were inspired by both Samuel Lee's *Orbis Miraculum* and John Bunyan's *Solomon's Temple Spiritualiz'd*, which appeared at about the same time. Speculative Masons, who were concerned with social respectability and had no desire to threaten the establishment, finally rejected the "Legend of the Craft" which honoured the Tower of Babel, a pagan edifice constructed in open defiance to heaven. Instead of the Promethean or Faustian Nemrod, they preferred "our wise King Solomon", or as *A Mason's Examination* of 1723 puts it: "Grand Master in his time of Masonry and Architecture."

Tracing board showing a scene from the legend in which King Hiram and Solomon are overheard by an eavesdropper. Eighteenth century.

This break with tradition is clearly illustrated in a 1725 catechism, entitled *The Whole Institutions of Free-Masons, Opened*, where the following passage occurs: "We are not like the Babylonians who thought to build up to the heavens, but we pray the Holy Trinity to enable us to built the True, the All Mighty and the Just, in praise of Him to whom all praise is due." The 1726 *Graham* manuscript, which is often quoted today by Freemasons who claim to be part of an "authentic tradition", repeats this idea, using almost exactly the same words.

However, it was in Solomon's Temple that the murder of Hiram the architect took place. A mystical tale has arisen around this incident. It speaks of a Lost Word, the word of life, key to all secrets, which was substituted at that time, as much because it was lost, as because such a word could not be spoken. As for "wise King Solomon", it was he who inspired Francis Bacon's *New Atlantis* which in turn influenced the founders of the Royal Society in 1662. This institution shares the Masons' "faith", as expressed in two essential ideas:

– all men are brothers and must be judged according to their good works, and not the religion they belong to;

– ignorance is the cause of all vice and of the evil men do to one another. The human species can be redeemed only through knowledge.

Jean Théophile Desaguliers (1683–1739), a friend of Newton and co-author with Anderson of the charter of modern Freemasonry (*Constitutions*, first version 1723), was an extremely active member of the Society. As Grand Master of the Grand Lodge of England, he declared himself for a "natural religion" which was above revealed beliefs. The son of a pastor from La Rochelle, who emigrated to England after the repeal of the Edict of Nantes in 1685, his own family history had proved to him the disastrous effects of a single imposed way of thinking. Solomon's temple, which was destroyed, rebuilt, then destroyed again, is the scene of a story which synthesises and symbolises all of history and each of our personal histories. This is why it provides Freemasons with so many useful pointers and illustrations, stimulating thoughts about the future of human mankind, for it is a place where possibility reigns, where promise and danger intertwine.

The first temple, which is described in the Bible (1 Kings 6,2), is the setting for the degree of Master, or that of Secret Master (fourth in the Ancient and Accepted Scottish Rite), of Intimate Secretary (the sixth degree), of Provost and Judge (the eighth degree), of Intendant of the Buildings (the eighth degree), and of the Grand Elect of the Sacred Vault (the fourteenth degree). The Royal Arch (in the English Rite) and the thirteenth degree of the Scottish Rite refer to it indirectly. The legend, which is specifically linked to these teachings, tells of how the three architects discovered the traces of an ancient temple attributed to Enoch while digging the foundations for the temple, and in these ruins found a brilliantly shining Triangle.

The temple of the Démophiles Lodge in Tours, France, which dates from the reign of Napoleon III (1852–70).

The second temple, built by Zerubbabel after his captivity in Babylon, is the setting of the capitulary degrees. The first of these is the Knight of the Orient or of the Sword (the fifteenth degree of the Ancient and Accepted Scottish Rite).

In each of these legendary locations, searchers act out different roles and internalise them, by testing themselves against the experiences of historical or mythical characters.

I. THE UNION CHAIN AND THE INDENTED TASSEL, THE KNOTTED ROPE AND THE LEMNISCATE

The Apprentices' tracing board is encircled by a knotted rope, as are the walls of the temple, although the rope does not reach right round it. At the two ends, near the pillars, there is a tassel. Rope is used by builders to trace out angles and straight lines, while the spaces between the knots represent units of measurement. It is important to distinguish the knotted rope from the indented tassel, a frieze of black and white triangles which runs around the lodge's tracing board.

The knots in the rope are not pulled tight, and form a sideways number 8, like the mathematical symbol for infinity. This sideways 8 is a geometric figure, called the lemniscate (from the Greek *lemniscatas*, adorned with ribbons) and formed by two joined slightly elliptical rings. One of its symbolic properties, termed "squarability", raises a number of questions. Squarability means that the area of one of the rings of the lemniscate is equal to the area of a square whose sides are the length of the diameter of the circle inscribed within a ring.

This construction represents the squaring of the circle. The properties of the lemniscate were studied by Bernouilli (1654–1705) after the work of Cassini (1625–1712), the first director of the Paris Observatory who discovered two of Saturn's satellites. The lemniscate matches the apparent orbit of the planets around the sun, as observed from the Earth. The real orbit is elliptical, and the apparent orbit of a planet whose orbit is elliptical traces a lemniscate.

This exploration of the links between appearance and reality is part of the passage from knowledge to experience.

The three columns topped with Ionic, Doric and Corinthian capitals symbolising Wisdom, Strength and Beauty.

CHAPTER 4

THE MOSAIC PAVEMENT

OPPOSITES UNITED

THE MOSAIC PAVEMENT, OR CHECKERED FLOOR, HAS BLACK AND WHITE SQUARES, LIKE A CHESSBOARD. IT CAN BE SEEN ON THE floor in the centre of the lodge where its role is to make us think about opposites, how they contradict and complement each other. Apprentices are generally asked to study this subject. Masonic texts of the eighteenth century refer to the mosaic pavement as "Moses' pavement" or "the lodge's marvellous floor". In Pritchard's *Masonry Dissected* (1730), the mosaic square is considered to be both the floor of the lodge and the paving stones of the temple. Other texts claim: "It is the tiling on which the high priest walked in Solomon's temple." However, this allusion can be disputed, for the mosaic pavement does not have Hebraic origins.

It first appeared in the first century B.C. in Rome. At that time, the term was used for mosaics decorating natural or artificial caves, and fountains. Dedicated to the Muses, the nine goddesses of the arts, such places of rest and relaxation were called *musaea*. The decorations found here were known as *musium opus*, abbreviated to *mussinum*. This is where the word mosaic comes from, not to be confused with Moses. In the past, a tracing board would be drawn on the floor with chalk when work began. The modern tracing board is a painted canvas, and since it is rolled out onto the floor, it is often referred to as the carpet. It shows all the Masonic objects in the temple: two pillars topped with pomegranates framing a piece of rough stone, called ashlar; a square stone with a point; the Moon and the Sun; a square and compasses; a plumb line; a plumb rule; a gavel and chisel; and the trestle board. Around these symbols is a knotted rope. This is what the tracing boards of Apprentices would generally look like, but they vary according to the different degrees and rites.

THE TRESTLE-BOARD

The trestle board (shown below) shows the symbols which make up the letters of the Masonic alphabet. Letters are inscribed in geometrical figures, which in the past were used for writing inscriptions but today generally play a decorative role.

  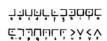

Each degree has its own tracing board, which shows the symbols of that grade.

CHAPTER 5

KING SOLOMON'S THRONE

THE MASTER'S CHAIR

"EAST OF EDEN" IS WHERE CAIN WAS MARRIED, BUILT A TOWN AND FOUNDED A DYNASTY OF CREATORS (GENESIS 4,16). IN THE EAST, WHERE the sun rises, the first murderer became the first builder.

This disturbing fact merits some consideration. The questions it raises lie at the very foundations of history. Light disturbs the order dreamt of in the darkness of oblivion. That is its function. The expression *lux ex tenebris* is current among Continental Freemasons. The darkness is pregnant with light and the builder is the midwife. The last descendant of Cain was Tubal-Cain, whose name means "the blacksmith of the Universe". The blacksmith is a man of knowledge who masters the four elements of earth, water, fire and air. He has a skill which can accomplish what knowledge only promises, ripping open the belly of the earth, extracting metals, forging tools and everything else he might want and need in order to become a king. He is, in effect, a practitioner of the "Royal Art", that is to say the art of becoming a free man, able to choose his destiny and become increasingly self-sufficient.

Work begins in the lodge with the lighting of candles, or lights. The lodge is thus lit up, but not flooded with sunlight, which would be as blinding as darkness. True knowledge involves an understanding of measurements and doses, what is enough and what is too much. The lodge is a place of light and shade so that everyone can catch a glimpse of the stars. This brings to mind a poem by Goethe, who was both a poet and a Freemason.

Gloom-embraced will lie no more,
By the flickering shades obscured,
But are seized by new desire,
To a higher union lured.

Then no distance holds you fast;
Winged, enchanted, on you fly,
Light your longing, and at last,
Moth, you meet the flame and die.

Never prompted to that quest:
Die and dare rebirth!
You remain a dreary guest
On our gloomy earth.[1]

1. Extract from "Blessed Longing", Goethe, *Roman Elegies and Other Poems*, translated by Michael Hamburger. Anvil Press Poetry, London, 1996.

The chair of the Worshipful Master, who presides over the work of the lodge.

The East, or the Orient, is also used to express the lodge's position. Thus each town which is to the east of the one where Freemasons are working is associated with the east of Eden. It was here that, according to the Bible, the first city was built. In France, for example, the term "Grand Orient" is used for a federation of lodges. Lodges lie on a west-east axis. The entrance is in the west and, in the east, facing the door, sits the Master in the Chair, also known as the Lodge Master or Worshipful Master. Since a lodge symbolically represents Solomon's temple, the Lodge Master sits on "King Solomon's throne".

The Mason's project is to create a "more just and more enlightened society" and discussing this subject many eighteenth-century Masonic texts point to ignorance as the principal root of evil. Spreading the light therefore was often expressed in the form of teaching or distributing books. Alexander Pushkin, the poet, and his brethren of the Ovid lodge, for example, used to go out after each meeting to hand out books—food for the soul—to the poorest homes in their city.

The eighteenth century was known as the Enlightenment, and during this period the overall vision of the world was humanistic: all men have the right to be happy and to choose their own destinies, whatever their births. Although the word humanism itself only became current from the time of the Renaissance in Europe, it is actually part of an extremely ancient tradition.

During the Enlightenment, all ways of thinking, whether mystical or philosophical, revolved around the idea that human beings can become perfect. Anderson's Masonic text *Constitutions* (1723), for example, suggests uniting people in a religion "in which all Men agree … that is, to be *good Men and true*". This implies the idea of a "natural" morality linked to a vision of Nature as good and reassuring. Enlightenment humanism incorporated and developed this image of a kind and benevolent Nature, like a mother who feeds her child. Painters such as Fragonard (1732–1806) depicted Nature as good and beautiful. The characters in his pictures frolic with voluptuous innocence, for what is natural cannot be perverse or evil. In the same way, ideas were considered less important than feelings and it was held that people should be judged according to their behaviour and not according to their beliefs or to what social, ethical or religious groups they belonged to.

Enlightenment humanism sets the "sweetness" of Nature against the rigidity of despotism and barbarity. Nature was idealised as the "bountiful mother", a term reminiscent of ancient initiation rites and of Demeter, Greek goddess of fertility. She was set against the hierarchies and the authority of the father.

This association of Nature and the mother is interesting also in connection with the Masonic myth of Hiram, the architect of Solomon's temple. The Bible presents this hero as being a widow's son, which is why masons call themselves "widow's children". Many founding fathers are called sons of widows or of virgins for this reason, and the implication is that the absence of a father sets them apart from or qualifies them as Creators.

Opposite: the gavel and the sword symbolise temporal and spiritual power.
Following double page: the Moon and the Sun represent the cosmogony
of the lodge and the passing from darkness to light.

CHAPTER 6

LIGHT

A METAPHOR FOR THE WORD

THE WORD LIGHT HAS A NUMBER OF SEPA-
RATE MEANINGS FOR FREEMASONS, WHICH
TOGETHER FORM A NETWORK OF MEANING
which expresses the breadth and depth of its
importance to their thinking.

I. MASONIC LIGHT
When a new member becomes a Freemason he is
"given the light" during the ceremony of initiation to the degree of Entered Apprentice. The
shock of initiation comes when the blindfold is
removed from his eyes.

II. THE THREE LESSER LIGHTS
These are the Sun, the Moon and the Lodge
Master, and are described in these terms: "The
Sun to rule over the day, the Moon to preside
over the night and the Master to govern and
direct his lodge."

III. THE THREE GREATER LIGHTS
These are "the volume of the sacred law, the
square and the compasses". The volume of the
sacred law is the Bible, open either at the Book of
Kings or at the first page of the Gospel According
to Saint John which reads: "In the beginning was
the Word." It can be any other book which is

recognised as being of great spiritual worth, thus
reflecting the fact that Freemasonry is open to
people of many religions, united by their belief in
a Supreme Being.

Such diversity is reassuring. For a library must
constantly be added to and the last book remains to
be written. If having no books is hardly a good
thing, what is worse is to have only one book and to
set it up as a fixed and unchanging monument.

IV. THE LIGHTS OF THE WORKSHOP
In the French and Scottish Rites, the Worshipful
Master (or Lodge Master), the two Wardens, the
Orator and the Secretary are called "the Lights of
the Workshop". Sometimes the term "the three
great lights" is used for the Worshipful Master and
the two Wardens. The symbolism of light and its
relationship with Enlightenment humanism has
already been dealt with in the chapter concerning
the Orient and the throne of King Solomon. In
the Memphis Rite, the temple is "lit with the
light of Egypt". The "light of freedom" is referred
to at the thirtieth degree of the Ancient and
Accepted Scottish Rite (that of Grand Elect
Knight Kadosh). In Belgium, the Sun, the Moon,
the Blazing Star and the Starry Vault are called
the "astral lights".

*The three-branched candlestick, used in Continental practice,
is brought out when the lodge starts its work.*

CHAPTER 7

THE VOLUME OF THE SACRED LAW

THE FIRST GREATER LIGHT

"THE VOLUME OF THE SACRED LAW", AS DESCRIBED IN THE PREVIOUS CHAPTER, MAY BE ANY BOOK OF IMPORTANCE TO THE individual or the lodge. It is generally the Bible, open at the relevant chapter of Kings, or else at the first page of the Gospel According to Saint John which reads: "In the beginning was the Word." It can be the holy book of the new members' religion, so that they can swear their oath on it: the *Qur'an*, the *Veda*, the *Bhagavad Gita*, the *Zend-Avesta*, the *Tao Te King*, or the *Constitutions* of Freemasonry.

A brief story helps our understanding here. A "searcher" goes out in quest of a place of enlightenment where he can attain true wisdom. When he finds one that suits his nature, he remains there, following the masters' teachings and adhering to their strict discipline. He stays for several years. When he has grown old, he decides to return home in order to teach what he has learnt to his family. He takes leave of his masters and asks them to give him a text containing the essence of their teachings, perhaps even in a hidden form, so that he can use it to refresh his memory whenever necessary. His request is accepted and he leaves satisfied. On the way home, he discovers that there is nothing written

on the precious scroll that he has been given. He returns to his masters and expresses his surprise. They answer: "We thought you were more advanced than that. Here, then, is a text containing signs. We have many of them, but generally give them only to beginners."

The ultimate book remains still to be written. He who becomes himself, and so lives a real life, needs blank pages in order to produce meaning, and not reproduce it. Books are to be read as a stimulus for conversation. Listening is a sterile activity if it does not lead to something previously unsaid.

That is why the notion of the sacred is a matter for study and debate for the Freemasons. Books considered to be sacred are there to be read. The act of reading entails not only receiving a message, but also understanding it, deciphering its metaphors and allegories, finding out where this version came from and wondering: "Who wrote this version and where is the original? Where do the copies come from?" Reading involves not only checking what the text says, but also what the commentators have said about it. The use of geometric analysis enlightens and guides the reader. Each book, sacred or not, adds its own flame, and light is made up of countless different flames.

In most Masonic lodges a sacred volume is placed on the pedestal. In this case, it is the Bible, open at the beginning of the Gospel according to Saint John.

ÉVANGILE DE NOTRE SEIGNEUR JÉSUS-CHRIST

SELON

SAINT JEAN.

CHAPITRE I.

Jésus-Christ est la Parole de Dieu faite chair. Jean-Baptiste lui rend témoignage. Il se fait connaître à André, à Pierre, à Philippe et à Nathanaël.

La *a* Parole était au commencement; *b* la Parole était avec Dieu, *c* et cette Parole était Dieu.

2 Elle était *d* au commencement avec Dieu.

3 *e* Toutes choses ont été faites par elle, et rien de ce qui a été fait n'a été fait sans elle.

4 *f* C'est en elle qu'était la vie, *g* et la vie était la lumière des hommes.

5 *h* Et la lumière luit dans les ténèbres, et les ténèbres ne l'ont point reçue.

6 *i* Il y eut un homme, appelé Jean, qui fut envoyé de Dieu.

7 *k* Il vint pour *être* témoin et pour rendre témoignage de la lumière, afin que tous crussent par lui.

8 Il n'était pas *lui-même* la lumière, mais *il était envoyé* pour rendre témoignage à la lumière.

9 *l* C'était là véritable lumière, qui éclaire tous les hommes en venant au monde.

10 Elle était dans le monde, *m* et le monde a été fait par elle; mais le monde ne l'a pas connue.

11 *n* Il est venu chez soi, et les siens ne l'ont point reçu.

12 *o* Mais à tous ceux qui l'ont reçu, il leur a donné le droit d'être faits enfants de Dieu; *savoir*, à ceux qui croient en son nom;

13 *p* qui ne sont point nés du sang, ni de la volonté de la chair, ni de la volonté de l'homme, mais qui sont nés de Dieu.

14 *q* Et la Parole a été faite chair, et a habité parmi nous, *r* pleine de grâce et de vérité; *s* et nous avons vu sa gloire, une gloire telle que celle du Fils unique venu du Père.

15 *t* C'est de lui que Jean rendit

témoignage, lorsqu'il criait : C'est ici celui dont je disais : *u* Celui qui vient après moi m'est préféré, parce qu'il est plus grand que moi.

16 *x* Et nous avons tous reçu de sa plénitude, et grâce sur grâce.

17 *y* Car la loi a été donnée par Moïse; *mais z* la grâce et *a* la vérité sont venues par Jésus-Christ.

18 *b* Personne ne vit jamais Dieu : *c* le Fils unique, qui est dans le sein du Père, est celui qui *nous* l'a fait connaître.

19 *d* C'est ici le témoignage que Jean rendit, lorsque les Juifs envoyèrent de Jérusalem des sacrificateurs et des Lévites pour lui demander : Qui es-tu?

20 Il *le* confessa, et ne *le* désavoua point; il *le* confessa, en disant : Je ne suis point le Christ.

21 Qu'es-tu donc? lui demandèrent-ils. *e* Es-tu Élie? Et il dit : Je ne le suis point. Es-tu *f* le prophète? Et il répondit : Non.

22 Ils lui dirent : Qui es-tu donc? afin que nous rendions réponse à ceux qui nous ont envoyés. Que dis-tu de toi-même?

23 *g* Il dit : Je suis la voix de celui qui crie dans le désert : Aplanissez le chemin du Seigneur, *h* comme a dit le prophète Ésaïe.

24 Or, ceux qui avaient été envoyés vers lui étaient d'entre les pharisiens.

25 Ils lui demandèrent encore : Pourquoi donc baptises-tu, si tu n'es point le Christ, ni Élie, ni le prophète?

26 Jean leur répondit, en leur dit : *i* Pour moi, je baptise d'eau; mais il y a au milieu de vous quelqu'un que vous ne connaissez point;

27 *k* C'est celui qui vient après moi, qui m'est préféré, et je ne suis pas digne de délier la courroie de ses souliers.

CHAPTER 8

THE TWO PILLARS

A SYMBOL OF DUALITY

THE TWO PILLARS MARK THE PASSAGE FROM ONE PLACE TO ANOTHER QUITE DIFFERENT ONE. THEY REPRESENT THE MYTHOLOGICAL Pillars of Hercules which were thought to stand at Gibraltar. They announce the departure from a familiar world to an unknown one.

The pillars at the door of the temple are purely ornamental and do not support the roof. Ancient temples often had two pillars. For example, the two obelisks at the entrance of the temple of Karnak are far older than the two pillars of Solomon's temple. Hiram, the architect chosen by King Solomon, came from Tyre where, according to Herodotus, two pillars stood in front of the temple of Hercules, "one of gold, the other of emerald".

Their symbolic nature is essentially binary: each of them represents one pole of reality. They are aesthetically similar, but each has its own particular character.

The pillars of Solomon's temple serve as signposts for Freemasons. The Apprentices sit facing the northern pillar, while the Fellows sit facing the southern one. Masters can sit wherever they like. Each pillar has its warden. The northern pillar has the Junior or New Warden, while the southern pillar has the Senior or Old Warden.

The pillars are described in three Biblical passages: 1 Kings 7, 15–21 and 2 Chronicles 3, 15–17 and 4, 11–13. All three descriptions, although markedly different, name the right-hand pillar Jachin and the left-hand one Boaz. What must be determined—and what is still questioned today—is whether right and left should be taken from the inside or outside of the building. In the Masonic rites, Jachin is translated as "may it establish" or "may it affirm" and Boaz as "with strength". The Hebrew word for pillar is *amoud* (plural *amoudim*), from the root letters *ayin*, *mêm* and *daleth* which means "to stand, to be upright, to be situated there". As for the symbolism of the letters, to which the cabbalists attached a great importance because they give life to the meaning of the words (a cabbalistic adage says: "let the letters in the words come alive"), it goes as follows: *ayin* is the eye, *mem* is the origin, water and mother, and *daleth* is the door.

Emulation Working, which is a commonly observed English system of Freemasonry, says of the pillars: "They were built to be hollow, so that they could hold the archives of Masonry and indeed the scrolls of the constitution were laid within them."

Eighteenth and nineteenth-century aprons were richly decorated with symbols. These included Solomon's temple, the two pillars, the Masonic pavement, the delta, the Moon and the Sun, as well as other tools appropriate to the grade of the apron's wearer.

Other rituals, notably the York Rite, which is commonly observed in the United States, affirm that: "They were built to be hollow in order to preserve the archives of Freemasonry from earthquakes and floods". In the *Constitutions* of 1738, James Anderson says this of them: "Some call them the pillars of Seth, but the old masons always refer to them as the pillars of Enoch." This remark is an allusion to the temple attributed to Enoch and mentioned in chapter 3 above.

I. THE THREE COLUMNS

In many rites, three columns topped with candles, or three tall candlesticks are placed in the lodge. Lights are lit at the beginning of work and extinguished at the end. These columns, or pillars, stand for the trinity of Wisdom-Strength-Beauty. Wisdom is necessary for invention, strength to accomplish a task and beauty is for ornament.

II. THE POMEGRANATES, LILIES AND SPHERES

The pillars are topped by capitals decorated with pomegranates, lilies and spheres. How many of them there are and how they are distributed depends on which of the Biblical passages mentioned above is referred to. This gives a creative license to modern artists.

Commentators on rituals have compared the seeds of the pomegranate to the Masons, who are joined together by their souls. In ancient Greece, pomegranate seeds were linked to the idea of error. Persephone tells her mother how she was seduced against her will: "He cunningly placed sweet sugared food in my hand, a pomegranate seed, and forced me to eat it despite myself" (Homeric Hymn to Demeter).

Is this a forbidden fruit then, like the one eaten by Eve? In the text of Genesis the fruit is not actually named. The word used is *peri*, which just means fruit. This has become apple in translation, but many commentators now associate the apple with the pomegranate. In fact, the fruit in Genesis could well be a fig or a pomegranate, which are more common in the Middle East than apples.

As for the lilies, Masonic symbolism is, here too, based on an arbitrary translation. The Biblical description of the pillars talks of *chochana*, which can be translated as rose. Johannis Buxtorfi's Hebrew-Latin dictionary, published in Amsterdam in 1654, translates *chochana* as *lilium*, the lily, as does the Vulgate, Saint Jerome's Latin translation of the Bible.

The pillars are also decorated with two spheres, one representing the earth and the other the sky. In Emulation Working, these spheres are placed on top of the small pillars, similar to those of the temple, placed on the Wardens' tables. When the lodge begins its work, the earth colonnette is laid flat and the sky colonnette upright. At the end of the work, it is necessary to "come back down to earth", so the order is reversed.

Opposite: ornament made by a press-ganged sailor showing a tracing board.
Following double page: letter standing for the Jachin pillar.
Letter standing for the Boaz pillar.

CHAPTER 9

THE BUILDER'S TOOLS

INCREASING THE POWER OF THE HANDS

THE SQUARE AND COMPASSES ARE INSTRU-MENTS OF GEOMETRY. THE FIRST KNOWN TEXTS WHICH TALK OF FREEMASONRY ARE the *Regius* and *Cooke* manuscripts of 1390 and 1425. These are the oldest of the texts known as "The Old Charges". They classify the different areas of knowledge and equate Freemasonry with geometry: "The fifth science is geometry, also known as Masonry. It is the art of measuring everything on Earth and in Heaven."

After the list of the seven liberal arts comes the following observation: "No science, not even grammar or rhetoric, can operate without geometry." This implies that geometry, the art of measuring as its etymology indicates, is far more than just the art of tracing figures, and of comparing their lengths, surfaces and volumes. The art of measuring in fact entails proof, and progress in this art teaches how to demonstrate the truth of a proposition by means of its tools, the set square and compasses.

In the Middle Ages, the teaching of geometry cleared the way for objective thought. Until that time, all knowledge had been handed down from an authority: an affirmation was considered to be true because it had been declared by priests who were recognised by the establishment. The expressions *Magister dixit* (The Master has said it) and *Roma locuta, causa finita* (Rome has spoken, the case is closed) were meant to put a stop to any debate and eliminate doubt or the need for proof. Only one kind of knowledge could not be taught in this way: geometry. A theory about the properties of a shape can only be accepted when it has been verified using reason, and a square and compasses.

The teaching of geometry implies therefore the recognition of students as people who are able to think rationally and find meaning on their own. Such teaching creates and structures critical faculties and objective analysis. Most importantly, it develops the desire to prove the truth of a proposition. Thus, the square and the compasses are essentially tools for verifying the truth of the matter.

The oldest definition of Freemasonry emphasises its central function and role in the city: a Mason is someone who proves by verification, that is to say someone who listens attentively to "what" is being said and not to "who" is saying it. The geometrician-builder measures words with the yard-stick of meaning and not according to the social status of the speaker.

The square and compasses, therefore, are

Emblems of the lodge.

the tools of a free man. They are the tools of a way of thinking which recognises the possibility of making statements about reality, understanding its laws and modifying it in order to better the human condition. They take the place of amulets and talismans in the wake of the development of a higher consciousness. The square and compasses have no intrinsic power. They are tools invented by human beings to help them exercise the power they know they possess to shape reality. Symbolism makes the meaning of these tools clearer by depicting them as images of the mind that conceived and created them. The square and compasses are symbolic to the extent that they represent in a material form the shape and skill of the human soul.   .

The square and compasses are also used to represent rational thought. This is, however, not understood merely as the ability to deduce and induce, without any assistance from intuition or imagination. To recognise one's faculties it is necessary to distinguish them. But, on the other hand, separating them off would be disastrous and unrealistic. Euclid's series of propositions offers a rational progression, in the strict sense of the term, but intuition and imagination must play their part. The step from one proposition to the next is not a simple matter of deductive logic, it is also an intuitive and imaginative leap.

In almost every tradition, the set square is associated with the geometric square, the Earth and matter; the compasses are linked to the circle, Heaven and the spirit.

Those who journey in search of truth must not be content just to memorise this point. Working with symbolism begins with the question "why?". It is necessary to analyse the meaning behind the relationship between spirit and circle, between square and matter. The search for this meaning casts light on how mental structures work. In the context of this exploration, psychology is more useful than metaphysics. The latter is, in fact, a construct, and hence an effect. Psychology can explore the elements of the construct, and hence its causes.

When beginning work as an Apprentice, the square is laid on top of the compasses to show that the spirit is still dominated by matter. At the second degree, that of Fellow, the square and compasses are interlaced. There is balance.

At the degree of master, the compasses are laid over the square.

I. THE GAVEL AND THE CHISEL

These two tools are used to impose the worker's will on a piece of stone. Masons strike their chisel with the gavel to create the shape that they have imagined. The gavel is thus associated with the active will. This explains why it is given to the Worshipful Master and the two Wardens. During a ritual, it is used to announce the beginning and the end of the work, and to request leave to speak. During the initiation ceremony, the Worshipful Master places the sword on the new member's shoulder then hits its blade with the gavel.

The gavel, derived from the Teutonic root *geb*, meaning "to give", is a double-headed wooden hammer.

A hand holding the stone-cutter's chisel symbolising the work which must be done on the self.

The chisel, from the Latin *cisellus*, the substantive form of the verb *cædere*, "to cut", is a small piece of hardened steel, sharpened at one end.

The fact that the gavel and chisel are useless for cutting stone individually, makes the complementary nature of the active and the passive quite clear. This is further brought out by the symbolic meanings associated with these two tools. The gavel is, of course, the active element because it hits the chisel, thus giving it a force which the passive chisel directs.

II. THE PLUMB LINE AND THE PLUMB RULE

The plumb line is a piece of lead on a string attached to a ring, while the plumb rule is a piece of lead on a line attached to the summit of a triangle. The former is used to find a vertical axis and the latter the horizontal axis.

Both of these two tools give the vertical axis, while the plumb rule is used to obtain the horizontal axis indirectly. The line of the plumb rule has to cross the base of the triangle and form a perpendicular, such that the triangle is divided into two identical right-angled triangles. The vertical axis is obtained by simply looking at the line when it is completely still. The horizontal axis can then be derived from it. A right angle must be created by adjusting the base of the triangle to the vertical line. The triangle is adjusted so that its base (the side facing the angle from which the line is suspended) forms a cross with the line. Gravity allows us to determine the vertical axis and, from that, determine the horizontal axis.

The study of these two tools suggests various metaphors which clarify how we locate ourselves on a vertical plane by determining its two dimensions, height and length.

III. THE GAUGE AND THE LEVER

The gauge and the lever are both straight lines. The gauge is a measuring tool, divided into twenty-four sections, like the division of the day into twenty-four hours, and allows us to check that the finished building conforms to the original plan. The number of sections on the gauge is divisible by two and by three, and is the product of the first four natural numbers (1 x 2 x 3 x 4). It is thus ideal for checking if proportions are correct.

The lever is a tool which increases the worker's physical strength. Everyone knows the challenge: "Give me but one firm spot on which to stand, and I will move the earth." It allows us to overcome the force of gravity. The lever is divided into two parts by its fulcrum, and it increases a man's strength in proportion to the length of the part he presses down on. This part is called "the power". The other, which is shorter and lies under the object to be lifted, is called "the resistance".

IV. THE TROWEL

This tool represents the final stage of a job, the moment when mortar or plaster is applied over the walls, thus obscuring the differences between the stones. It is also associated with creative power, which is illustrated by the fact that in the Middle Ages the Creator was sometimes depicted

Opposite: a hand holding the hammer symbolising a stone-cutter at work.
Following double page: the decoration at the centre of a lodge's banner, showing the tools of a building site where masons work.

holding a trowel. The symbolism of this tool is also based on its triangular blade and its jagged edge which looks like a bolt of lightning.

V. THE ROUGH ASHLAR, THE CUBICAL STONE AND THE POINTED CUBICAL STONE

Rough ashlar, or unhewn stone, is the raw material to be worked on. Stone symbolises human beings in their natural state, before they work on themselves through introspection. All writers agree on this view of rough ashlar as imperfect humanity. The symbolism of builders, guildsmen and Freemasons develops around the notion that "to make" refers to "making something of oneself". We need to consider the activity of working "on" unhewn stone, a Masonic expression which stands for introspection and self-improvement. Is it a question of forming identical stones, according to a pre-established pattern, so that they will fit perfectly together and form a pyramid? Or is it not rather a question of individualisation, during which process everyone discovers their particular self, getting rid of base "metals", which represent the prejudices we have about the outside world? A reading of Masonic texts shows that role models are presented with the invitation that they be copied. The models masons are asked to identify themselves with are the sages and, to achieve mastership, the architect Hiram. But, these same texts also contain countless injunctions to differentiate oneself rather than conform, to construct a new self, to enrich the group qualitatively rather than quantitatively.

Cutting stone is seen as a "becoming". It is an act which recognises the need for change. The uninitiated are full of metals that speak for them. When rid of these metals, the initiated can speak for themselves. The square of a square, the cube, has the same symbolism in three dimensions as the square does in two. It is an intrinsic part of the material world and the four elements. Its appearance is identical no matter which face it stands on, which is why it is associated with stability. On the other hand, the pointed cubical stone is a cube topped with a pyramid; it can be set down only on the face opposite the pyramid. Oswald Wirth says of it: "This tool, which masons have borrowed from carpenters, clearly shows that a stone must be split open so that its inner esotericism can be discovered."

The ancient English texts refer to "free-stone", a soft chalky rock which builders used for carving figures. The hard stone used for large-scale work was called "rough-stone". According to certain authors, the etymology of the word Freemason is "free-stone Mason". For others, the word was first used to describe a serf who was "freed" due to his skills as a Mason, and thus was allowed to travel as he pleased. Perhaps it comes from the association between the softness of free-stone and the ideal of personal freedom.

Free-stone encourages the freedom of the Mason because it is easy to carve. It puts up no resistance, but readily adopts the form which the person working it desires. The softness of the stone sets the Mason free.

A painted lambskin apron of English origin (early nineteenth century), representing the three holy virtues, Faith, Hope and Charity.

CHAPTER 10

THE MASON'S CLOTHING

DRESSED FOR WORK

FREEMASONS DRESS TO TAKE PART IN THE WORK OF THE LODGE. WITH AN APRON OVER THEIR EVERYDAY CLOTHES, AND GLOVES ON their hands, they are ready for the opening ceremony. Depending on their degree and rite, they may also wear a sash or collar. At the beginning dress was simple, thus conforming to the philosophy of the Craft, which required that its members put all superficiality behind them. But the eighteenth century witnessed a burgeoning taste for luxury, as princes and commoners started to fraternise in the lodges. A whole industry grew up, providing an enormous range of articles of all kinds.

I. THE APRON

The apron, the Masons' most distinctive item of clothing, is considered a tool. It goes back to the days of working Masonry, when masons wore a long apron of thick leather to protect themselves against splinters of rock and blows from their tools. Entered Apprentices' aprons are made of a white hide, traditionally lambskin. The triangular bib or flap is raised up. The Fellows wear the same apron, but with the bib turned down. Masters' aprons are made of hide or satin, edged with red, green or blue depending on the rite,

and lined with black. As a piece of protective clothing, the apron symbolises hard work because it is necessary to protect oneself from splinters of rough ashlar. At the same time it helps create and maintain the bond of belonging to the same fraternity.

II. THE SASH

The sash (worn by Continental and Scottish Masons) and collar are the only decorative items to be worn above the belt.

Their origin lies in the desire to show that all masons are equal. In pre-revolutionary France, the sash was worn only by the nobility. The Masonic lodge became the first place where everyone, whatever their social status or origins, wore a sash, showing equality from "on high". A privilege had been shared, rather than suppressed. The collar is a ribbon indicating an official position or a degree of initiation. A collar cannot be worn at the same time as a sash.

III. THE GLOVES

Gloves are generally white but, in the higher grades, may be red, black or white edged with red. At the beginning of Speculative Freemasonry, masons used to wear a sheet of vellum

A pair of gloves given to an apprentice during initiation.
Following double page: aprons (eighteenth century), belonging to Helvetius and
Voltaire, illustrating the symbols and legends associated with different Masonic degrees.

decorated with Masonic symbols instead of gloves. In the past, following the initiation ceremony, an Apprentice received two pairs of gloves: one for himself and another to give to "the lady he esteemed most highly". Nowadays, the second pair of gloves which was meant as a gift, has generally been replaced by a rose.

In 1780, having "been given the light" at the Amalia with Three Roses Lodge in Weimar, Goethe sent a pair of gloves to Madame de Stein with a letter containing the following words: "Here is a rather modest present, but it is one that a man can give only once in his life."

IV. THE HAT

In the eighteenth century, and for much of the nineteenth, the Worshipful Master wore a hat in the lodge, as did the Masters sometimes. This custom is still current among some Masters when they meet alone together in the Middle Chamber. The hat, like the crown, is an emblem of royalty and is associated with the Kether sephira in the cabbalistic Tree of Life. It is there as a reminder to the masters that their task is to rule, and not to wield power for their own purposes. This is a collective ideal, the shining diadem, and must have once been reminiscent of the Worshipful Master's tricorn. This figure is not a leader, in the sense in which the term is used in the outside world. The Worshipful Masters transmit what they receive and take part in a project which surpasses them. In Germany, all the brethren work with hats on, but uncover their heads whenever the Great Architect is referred to.

V. ROBES AND CHASUBLES

The dinner jacket is common in England, where it is used to establish a sense of harmony and symbolises equality. In Germany, meetings are conducted in tail coats and top hats.

The sisters of the Grand Female Lodge put a long black robe over their clothes at the beginning of the work. In the body of Memphis and the Swiss lodges of the Federation of Human Duty it is white. Female lodges in the Memphis Rite wear orange robes. In some lodges that observe the Rectified Scottish Rite, the men wear a blue chasuble.

Opposite: Master Masons wear sashes and Wardens wear collars decorated with the symbols of their offices.
Following double page: portrait of Prince Frederick of Holland (1797–1881), dressed as Grand Master.
"Lodge of Adoption" sash worn by Caroline Murat, Queen of Naples (1782–1839).

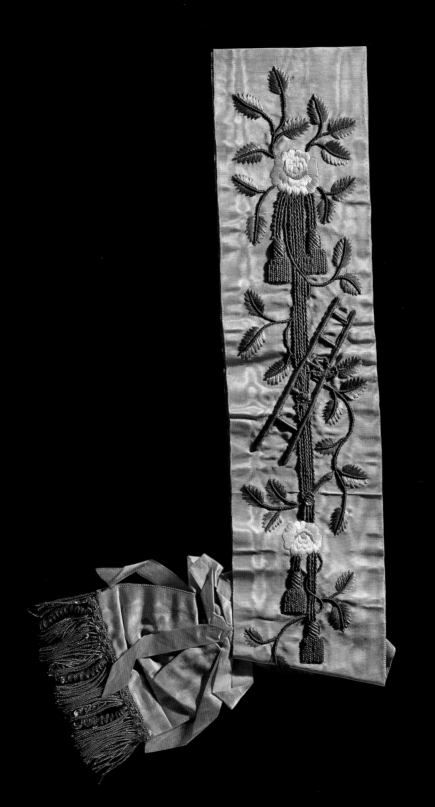

CHAPTER 11

THE BLADES

THE CUT AND THRUST OF CLEAR THINKING

THE INTRODUCTION OF SWORDS AND KNIVES INTO FREEMASONRY CAME ABOUT THROUGH SEVERAL DIFFERENT TRADITIONS: ANCIENT chivalry, with its legendary magic swords (for example, Excalibur); the Bible which, in the Book of Genesis, talks of a "flaming sword"; and the Freemasons themselves who, in the eighteenth century when swords were a sign of nobility, all wore them to show that they were equal and that nobility was a question of deeds and not of birth.

The straight-bladed sword has two cutting edges and a handle in the shape of a cross. All the members of a lodge have a sword, which they use during ceremonies. The curve-edged sword is known as "the flaming sword" due to its shape. This is an allusion to Genesis 3, 23–24: "He banished the man, and in front of the garden of Eden he posted the great winged creatures and the fiery flashing sword, to guard the way to the tree of life." The flaming sword is held by the Worshipful Master (the president of the lodge) during initiations to the grade of Apprentice, and is laid on his tracing board while the lodge works. It represents the Word, thought and creation. The dagger appears various times during a Mason's progression through the ranks: for the first time at the first degree, called "Vengeance"; and then at the ninth degree of the Ancient and Accepted Scottish Rite, called the Master Elect of Nine. The history of the dagger sheds light on its symbolism. Daggers have existed since neolithic times right through to the present day. They are thrusting weapons, designed for stabbing, and have a double-edged blade. In neolithic times the short blades, between 8 and 16 inches long, were made of stone and had already been so perfected that the metal blades that were later made of copper, bronze or iron, followed the same pattern. The blacksmith's art made longer blades possible, and so daggers became swords which are both thrusting and cutting weapons, allowing up and down blows. To understand the symbolic connotations of these weapons it is, then, vital to distinguish clearly between the sword and the dagger, between the act of cutting, slicing or splitting and the act of piercing. The dagger can be seen as a symbol of that which pierces a mystery, a secret, words and enigmas, allowing meaning to gush forth. In this way a weapon becomes a tool for thought. Polemus and Epistemes showed each other their reflections ... and discovered that they were twin brothers.

Opposite: hunting dagger with Masonic symbols, engraved by Joan Van der Nany in 1771.
Following double page: lodge swords, used in all ceremonies.

CHAPTER 12

THE VEGETABLE WORLD

FOOD, SIGNS AND ATTRIBUTES

THE SYMBOLISM OF THE VEGETABLE KINGDOM HARKS BACK TO THE BEGINNINGS OF SPEECH AND THOUGHT. EARLY DISCUSSIONS ABOUT Nature used the imagery of the human body: Mother Nature is fertilised by the rain, the seed of the Sky-Father, and lives an endless return through the cycles of the seasons. This created a set of metaphors which helped us place ourselves within the world. Soon after this type of metaphor came into existence, human beings began observing natural phenomena, and this study soon developed in opposition to mythological representations. Logos and Mythos then became conceptualised as two distinct categories which were opposed but complementary. The most ancient rites of all dwell on the cycle of death and resurrection. In every civilisation this was a way of structuring the important moments in a human life: birth, maturity and transformation. Masonic symbolism emphasises change and metamorphosis, and makes its own use of vegetable symbols. Freemasonry takes the essential part of its symbolic references from the world of minerals. Stone is both the medium and the raw material to be worked on, which is the task that builders' tools were designed for. But, in the eighteenth century, there also existed a Freemasonry of

wood with its own appropriate tools, in particular the axe. Forest rituals were practiced by guilds of carpenters, some of which have been retained by the stone Freemasons during their celebration of Midsummer Night.

The following exposition of vegetable symbolism occurs in the light of rites practiced by stone Freemasons.

I. THE CORN SEED

It is at the second degree, as a Fellow, that Freemasons discover the symbolism of the corn seed. This is introduced in a set of teachings related to the five senses, which we use to communicate. The death and rebirth of a seed is a theme common to most of the mystery cults of antiquity, particularly that of Eleusis. For the Egyptians, the ear of corn was the emblem of Osiris and symbolised his death and resurrection. It is important to remember in this context that Freemasons call themselves "children of the widow", an allusion to Hiram the architect who was "the son of a widow". The oldest known reference to "the son of the widow" occurs in an inscription on a tablet found in the pyramid of Cheops and refers to Horus, Osiris's posthumous child. A study of both sacred and secular ancient

Corn is part of the symbolism associated with the grade of Fellow.

texts reveals that a fatherless child, the son of a widow or of a virgin, always stands for a founder or creator.

II. THE ACACIA

The acacia appears at the third degree, that of Master, in the tale of the murder of Hiram the architect by his three impatient companions.

In *Masonry Dissected* (1730), Samuel Pritchard compares details of the story of the murder of Hiram with Aeneas's search for his father Anchises in the Sixth Book of Virgil's *Aeneid*.

Aeneas consulted the Sibyl to find out if he could go down among the shadows and talk with his father. The Pythoness gave him the necessary encouragement, but told him that he would succeed in finding his father Anchises, the ancestor of the Trojans, only if he plucked the Golden Bough and kept it in his hand. This Golden Bough could be pulled off its tree with ease. Similarly, Hiram is discovered under a branch of acacia, which comes away easily from the recently disturbed earth.

Virgil also tells a story which repeats some of the elements of Hiram's. Priam, the King of Troy, sent his son Polydorus to take a large sum of money to the King of Thrace. The Thracians killed Polydorus and buried him in secret. By chance, Aeneas was travelling through that country and pulled up the branch of a bush, so discovering the remains of Polydorus.

There is a common element in these stories: the effortless tearing up of a branch, which suggests that it had been uprooted elsewhere and replanted in the place where the dead man had been buried. This transplantation may be linked to a funeral rite, a basic rite which would have been provided even for a corpse that had been buried in secret.

The acacia grows in the desert and has extremely hard wood and dense thorns on its branches. Its name in Hebrew is *shita* (*sîn, têth, he*). There are three references to it in the Bible: once as a tree in Isaiah 41,19; as wood in Exodus 26, 26; and in the plural in Exodus 25, 5–37 which deals with the construction of the tabernacle.

III. THE TREE AND THE FOREST

When initiated into the twenty-second degree of the Ancient and Accepted Scottish Rite, the candidate becomes the Prince of the Lebanon or Royal Axe. The legend of this degree derives from the Bible and from the Arthurian cycles. The theme of building with wood comes from the Bible: Noah's ark and the Ark of the Covenant are the first and second temples. As for the Arthurian cycle of stories, it contributes the Round Table, which King Arthur made in order to stop his knights arguing about precedence.

This is what Paul Naudon and Edmond Gloton have to say about the subject:

"The legend of this grade teaches us that the Sidonians cut down the cedars of Mount Lebanon for the construction of Noah's ark. Their descendants did the same to make the Ark of the Covenant. This explains why they were also employed to supply the wood needed for the

Acacia, used for locating the tomb of Hiram the Master, and for building Solomon's temple.

75

building of Solomon's temple. Later, Zerubbabel was to use them again for the construction of the second temple. The extremely hermetic, esoteric teaching of this grade is the apotheosis of work carried out to make the Philosopher's Stone."[1]

This describes a metamorphosis, a progressive birth, the fruit of work performed on wood, on that vegetable matter which drinks the water kept in the earth, which grows and produces leaves and fruit that are edible for human beings, which burns in the fire and renews itself. The Ark of the Covenant, which was made of wood, sheltered the stone tablets of the Law. The temple was made of wood and stone. Work is an apprenticeship in the mastery of the mineral and vegetable worlds. Such work on an object, on "exterior" nature, is analogous to work on a subject, on "interior" nature.

The tree communicates. It is full of eloquent symbols for those who wish to put the act of becoming into words: the many branches stemming from a single trunk; the roots whose depth is proportional to the height of the trunk and to the extent and richness of its crown. It is a central metaphor for many cultures: the tree of the knowledge of good and evil, the tree of life, the axis of the world, the link between heaven and earth ...

But all that is well known and often repeated. What is important is to recognise a tree from its flowers and fruit, and not from its bark. This work is connected with the re-establishment of the living word, where conventional misunderstandings emphasise the importance of the bark, symbolising appearances or clothing. It is important to rediscover the true discourse which asks us to look at its flowers and fruit instead.

The journey from the forest to the stately hall containing the Round Table (whose shape abolishes any rank and around which sit only "peers") is clearly alluded to in the eighteenth-century ritual of the "Brethren of Charcoal-Burners" as recounted by Jacques Brengues:

"Where do you come from?
- From a forest.
- Where are you going, good brother?
- To the room of state.
- What will you do there?
- Overcome my passions, submit my will and learn the respectable trade of the charcoal-burners.
- What have you brought?
- Some wood, some leaves, some earth; to build, to strike, to cook in the furnace.
- Have you brought nothing else?
- I have also brought faith, hope and charity for all the brethren in the room of state.
- Who is that person you are leading?
- A man whom I found lost in the forest.
- What does he want?
- He wishes to learn the duties of a respectable charcoal-burner and to become a member of our order."[2]

The teaching of work is defined by a project: the making of the Philosopher's Stone. The journeymen of France, the brotherhood of char-

A rose, the alchemical symbol of life.

coal-burners and the Freemasons all live with this desire. And the conclusion will be the re-building of the temple and the arrival of a better, more enlightened society, symbolised by the Round Table, which abolishes places of honour. Initiates are experienced people and do not need leaders. If the assembly does have a president, that president is still an equal.

IV. THE LAUREL AND THE OLIVE

These two trees appear at the degree of Secret Master, the fourth in the Ancient and Accepted Scottish Rite.

A beautiful youth pursues a nymph who turns herself into a laurel tree in order to escape from him. This is the story of Apollo and Daphne, one of western art's favourite subjects.

Sacred to Apollo, the laurel tree symbolis-es victory in a literary competition or in a war. A wreath of its leaves was placed on the brows of victorious Roman generals, and later of emper-ors. This association comes from the fact that, like all evergreens, laurel is linked to the symbol-ism of immortality. It has a similar meaning in China, where the moon is said to contain one laurel tree and one immortal. As Apollo's tree, it brings together the wise man and the hero. In Greece, the Pythoness and her priests chewed or burned laurel leaves which, being sacred to Apollo, had divinatory powers. Those who received a favourable answer from the Pythoness returned home wearing laurel wreaths.

The olive tree is sacred to Athena. It grew in abundance on the plain of Eleusis, where it was protected. Anybody who damaged an olive tree was taken to court. It was given divine status in the Homeric *Hymn to Demeter*, which intro-duced initiates in to the mysteries of Eleusis.[3] In the Judæo-Christian tradition the olive tree is a symbol of peace. The dove brings an olive branch to Noah at the end of the flood and some legends relate that the Cross was made of olive and cedar wood. In the language of the Middle Ages it was a symbol of gold and of love. "If I can see gilded olive wood at your door, I shall then call you the temple of God", wrote Angelus Silesius, taking his inspiration from the descrip-tion of Solomon's temple.

Olive trees are found everywhere along the shores of the Mediterranean. Harvesting olives and making them into oil goes back to ancient times. The symbolism of the olive tree is thus rich in archaic experiences. Since olive oil was used to feed lamps, the tree is associated with light and, in the Islamic tradition, is called the "Blessed Tree", or the "Central Tree", meaning the axis of the world. It is useful to consider how the laurel and the olive tree are brought together in two ways. On the one had, the symbolic meaning of each may be added to that of the other in the belief that they then offer the sum of their symbolic content. On the other hand, they join to form a "symbolic couple", with a life of its own—nurtured, of course, by the symbolism of each separate element—but whose very exis-tence, especially in view of their relationship, forces us to choose, separate and develop. Before going any further, it should also be pointed out

Symbol of the Rose-Croix grade, embroidered on an eighteenth-century apron.

that the olive tree, like the laurel, is associated with victory. This is a common factor in their respective symbolism. The Greeks offered crowns of olive leaves to winners in the Olympic Games.

If these two trees have been brought together to show that the most important thing is their similarity, then the Secret Master must now meditate on the reward which follows effort. Without rejecting that possibility, the laurel-olive nexus also links Apollo and Athena. By studying the Apollo-Athena couple, we can penetrate into the "beginning" of thought (its architect) and find the road which leads us to an understanding of the relationship between effort and reward.

V. THE ROSE

The rose and its worship is central to European culture. It holds the same symbolic value as the lotus in the East. In the West, the rose is sacred to Aphrodite (Venus). It was born from Cupid's smiles, or fell from Aurora's hair as it was being combed. The first rose bush is supposed to have shot up from the ground as Venus emerged from the waves. A drop of nectar, the drink of the gods, fell on it and gave birth to the rose flower. According to legend, roses were originally white but, when Venus ran to help Adonis, who was being threatened by jealous Mars, a thorn stuck in her foot and the blood from the wound poured over the rose's white petals, dyeing them red. The Ass of Apuleius regains his human form by eating a garland of vermillion roses given to him by the High Priest of Isis. Thus, according to Apuleius,

the rose tree is a symbol of regeneration.

In sacred texts, the rose is often found together with the olive tree, which confirms the preceding interpretation. We read, for example, in Ecclesiasticus (24,14): "I have grown tall ... as the rose bushes of Jericho; as a fine olive in the plain."

The rose is also associated with knowledge and is thought to be the treasure of wisdom. Jean de Meung's *Roman de la Rose* is our first encyclopedia, the sum of thirteenth-century mediaeval knowledge. The "alchemical" or "mystic rose", personified in Christianity by the Virgin, should also be understood as a symbol of knowledge. The mystic rose is the final illumination at the last stage of a spiritual quest.

The rose represents wisdom, beauty and regeneration. Love transforms us by a process of metamorphosis. But these transformations are not necessarily beneficial and in this sense the myth of Circe can be read as a clear allegory. This dangerous sorceress transforms Ulysses's companions into swine because, unlike their leader, they are incapable of remaining clear-headed and wise during their orgy of drinking.

1. P. Naudon, *Histoire et Rituels des Hauts Grades maçonniques*. Paris, 1967. E. Gloton, *Mémento des grades capitulaires*. Paris, 1946.
2. J. Brengues, *La Franc-Maçonnerie du Bois*. Paris, 1973.
3. D. Béresniak, "Ce que nous savons des mystères d'Eleusis". *Le Maillon*, n°48, Nov. 1994.

Laurel stands for victories over oneself.

CHAPTER 13

THE ANIMAL WORLD

IMAGES FOR HUMANKIND

THE MASONIC RITES SET ASIDE SPECIAL PLACES IN THE CITY FOR MASTER MASONS WHO, HAVING LIVED THROUGH THE PASSION of Hiram, now work on other legends. In such places characters from the Bible encounter Olympians, Egyptians, Knights, temple builders and Faustian, or Promethean characters. In this collection of remembered images we discover our shared memory, the roots which give our experiences meaning. Real and imaginary animals take, naturally, their place these images.

I. THE TWO-HEADED EAGLE

This Hittite symbol (according to Frazer) was adopted by the Seleucid Turks during the Middle Ages. The crusaders learnt of it and adopted it in their turn. This symbol is, therefore, an example of what the West takes from the East.

Having first served as a symbol for the Austrian and Russian imperial armies, the two-headed eagle now represents every supreme council in the world. This is because it represents the dual nature of Unity. Once the traveller has reached the camp of the Kadosh, the bicephalous eagle will always remain with him. At this degree, it is black and white. At the thirty-third degree, it becomes completely black, while the

traveller is decked in white. During the final degrees of the rite, the double-headed eagle becomes more and more a symbol of power.

II. THE BRAZEN SERPENT
AND THE TRUE WORD

The brazen serpent appears at the twenty-fifth degree of the Ancient and Accepted Scottish Rite, the so-called Knight of the Brazen Serpent. To understand these words, it is enough to listen to their sound. The root letters *nûn, kaph, sîn* give the word *nahash*, meaning serpent, and also *nahash*, meaning omen. But these two words are not true homophones, because although the root letters are the same, their vowel sounds are different. The "a" of *nahash* (divination, omen) is a *pathah*, a shorter sound than the *qameç* which vocalises the "a" of *nahash* (serpent). The same root gives the verb *nahoch*, which means to practice the art of divination. The omen sense of these root letters is found in the Book of Numbers 23, 23 and 24, 1. *Nahash* vocalised as a serpent is also a proper noun, name of a king of the Ammonites and contemporary of Saul and David (1 Samuel 11, 1 and 2 Samuel 17, 25). We are told that he was the father of David's sister, Abigail, which implies, given that David's

Collar of the Prince of the Royal Secret, the thirty-second degree of the Ancient and Accepted Scottish Rite.

father was Jesse, that David and his sister had only one parent in common, their mother. Derived from this root is *nahoshet*, with the same spelling plus the feminising *taw* suffix, which means copper, as well as brass and bronze, two alloys whose main ingredient is copper. The legendary serpent of brass is called *Nahash nahoshet* (Numbers 21, 9) and was later to become an object of worship by the Israelites, who called it Nehushtan and made offerings of incense to it. It was then destroyed by King Hezekiah, a descendant of David (2 Kings 18, 3–5).

It should be noted that, without the suffix, the same letters *nûn, kaph, sîn,* vocalised *nahash,* are used in Ezekial 16, 36, to mean menstrual blood in the passage where he curses the whore. The first appearance of a serpent, or snake in the Bible is in the third chapter of Genesis. He predicts what will happen when Adam and Eve have tasted the fruit from the forbidden tree. It should be remembered that the first verse of this chapter says "Now, the snake was the most naked of all the wild animals", and that in nearly every official translation the word naked (*aroum*) is wrongly translated as shrewd or subtle.

Its nakedness represents the fact that it hides nothing, that it shows its true nature, that it does not lie. As for the serpent of brass, called *Nehushtan,* it was kept by the Israelites after the first temple had been built. It was placed in the courtyard of the temple and the people, believing that it could heal the sick, sacrificed animals to it.

III. THE PELICAN AND THE PHOENIX

These two animals are associated in Masonic symbolism. The former is represented feeding its young with its own flesh and blood; the latter rising from its own ashes. Love which is capable of self-sacrifice is connected with knowledge, transference and the renewal of generations. Blood is seen as the tonic of life. The pelican and the phoenix are depicted on the aprons and ornaments of the eighteenth degree, called the Rose-Croix Knight or Rose-Croix Prince, depending on the rite

IV. THE LAMB

The lamb is the original sacrificial victim in the world's three monotheistic religions (Judaism, Catholicism, Islam) and, even further back, in the Dionysian mystery cults. It also appears in the Hindu *Bhagavad Gita*, where it is associated with Krishna's interlocutor Arjuna, who rides on the back of a ram, and with the light at the centre of life.

In the Masonic rites, the lamb is represented at the seventeenth degree of the Ancient and Accepted Scottish Rite (the Knight of the East and West), lying on the scroll of seven seals, an image from Saint John's Revelation. At the eighteenth degree (the Rose Croix), the yearly banquet includes a lamb, whose flesh is eaten while its bones are ceremoniously burned. At the fourth degree of the Rectified Scottish Rite (the Scottish Master of Saint Andrew), the tracing board shows the slaughtered lamb and the celestial city of Jerusalem.

Opposite: the pelican feeding its young with its own entrails is an alchemical symbol of the Rose-Croix grade.
Following double page: the hive and its bees symbolize the work of the lodge.
The serpent which encircles the world is often depicted as Uroburos (the snake which bites its own tail).

V. THE IVORY KEY

The ivory key, the emblem of the Secret Master, has its place among the animal symbols since it is made of organic matter and is therefore different from the Masons' tools. Tools are made from minerals and vegetable matter, but the ivory key is not a tool. It is a sign. It represents its bearer's intention of opening his or her own interior locks to discover the future initiate in the depths where the master's body lies rotting.

A key in Hebrew is *mafteash*, from the root letters *pe* (or *phe*), *taw* and *kaph*. This etymology leads back to the Egyptian god Ptah, god of associations, exchange and creation. Ptah, the potter god, who was later associated by the Greeks with Hermes, was seen as being the master of artisans and scribes. He is the god of knowledge and creation. Pythagoras and many other Greeks went to Egypt to follow the teaching of the priests of Ptah. The name Pythagoras is itself a mystical name of Egyptian origin which phonetically reproduces in Greek the first words of the prayer to Ptah: P-T-Fh-Gh-R (Egyptian hieroglyphs, like Hebrew, were written without vowels). This inscription means "Ptah is great" or "the greatest", as Gardiner points out in his famous grammar.[1]

The ivory key is also connected with Pythagorism and the sources of Pythagorism, which lie in Memphis and the "white walls" of Ptah's temple. The oldest known text of Memphite teachings is a copy which the Egyptian king Shabaka made on black granite of a text which had, so it was said, been destroyed by worms. This text could well go back to the earliest dynasties: "It is Ptah who is called by the great name Tatenen ... he who fathered Atum, he who created the company of nine *neter*."[2] This text continues with the story of the death of Osiris and describes Ptah as the creator: "The great Ptah is the heart and tongue of the nine *neter*". It so happens that the Ancient and Accepted Scottish Rite teaches the symbolism of the ennead (the group of nine) at the fourth degree, whose emblem is the ivory key.

1. Sir Alan Gardiner, *Egyptian grammar, being an introduction to the study of hieroglyphs*, 3rd edition. Oxford University Press, 1973.
2. The Hebrew root *ntr* has a set of different nuances, such as "to undo", "to untie", "to release" and "to withdraw". Vocalised as *neter* it means natron, the native sesquicarbonate of soda which occurs in solution or as a deposit, mixed with other substances. As a metaphor, it stands for what is produced by dissolving.

Crowned compasses placed over the arc of a circle, inscribed with a Masonic alphabet, and linked by a rose on a cross and the phœnix, symbol of rebirth. Rose-Croix jewelry, eighteenth century.

THE WORLD AND NATURE

NATURE IS THE OTHER GREAT BOOK

IN ALL TRADITIONS, THE TEMPLE IS THE MEDI-
ATOR BETWEEN THE UNIVERSE AS MACRO-
COSM AND HUMAN BEINGS AS MICROCOSM.
That is why the Masonic temple depicts the Sun
and Moon on its east wall, the blazing star on its
west wall and the "starry vault" on its ceiling.
The Freemason passes through a number of specific natural locations during his journey of initiation.

I. THE CAVE

The cave's first appearance is at the ninth degree
of the Ancient and Accepted Scottish Rite (the
Master Elect of Nine) as the hiding place of the
murderer. The Hebrew language associates the
cave with a hole and with the eye socket of a
skull. The Hebrew root letters which contain
these meanings are *kaph* and *rês*, and the word
meaning cave, hole and eye socket is pronounced
khor or *khour*, the root being vocalised either
with an "o" or an "ou". *Khor* is also the Hebrew
form of the Egyptian god Horus, Isis and Osiris's
posthumous son who, in the pyramid versions of
the legend of Isis, is called "the child of the
widow".

    The association between cave and cavity
(as a hole or eye socket) exists in many languages,
including English. Perhaps it is universal? Its
symbolism must then be approached through this
association.

II. FIELDS, MOUNTAINS AND FORESTS

There is a degree at which the Freemason works
with nature. The walls of the temple are decorated with fields, mountains and forests, rivers and
waterfalls. At this degree, fresh questions are
asked concerning everything that has been learnt
about Masonic symbols, and the aim of this work
is, as the ritual puts it, "to search for the truth".
This is the twenty-eighth degree of the Ancient
and Accepted Scottish Rite, called the Knight of
the Sun or the Prince Adept. The great
American Mason, Albert Pike (1809–91), was
particularly fond of this degree. He wrote the
longest book ever published about the rite,
Morals and Dogma, which is known as the "Bible
of the Scottish Rite". Of the book's eight hundred pages, two hundred and twenty of them are
consecrated to the Knight of the Sun.

    To understand why Albert Pike attached
such a great importance to this teaching, it is
necessary to know about his own initiatory journey through the course of an adventurous life.
For a long time he lived among the Native

The acacia is one of the vegetable symbols which accompanies a Mason's life as an initiate.

Americans of Arkansas and Oklahoma. He learnt the languages of the Creek, Crow and Cherokee and taught in a school hidden away in the middle of the woods, before becoming a lawyer, fighting alongside the Confederates and rising as a Mason to be the Sovereign Grand Commander of the Ancient and Accepted Scottish Rite. The thinking of Native Americans is very close to the teaching of the Knight of the Sun. Albert Pike added a Native American element to it, and so enriched the Masonic tradition. This is justified by the Masons' notion of "gathering what is scattered" and also because a tradition is a form of memory which allows us to innovate. Native American rituals are not part of an organised religion, but take the form of "encounters". Thus, they do not transmit any dogmatic teachings, do not have any claims to an eternal truth, but allow an exchange of ideas and impressions. That is why the Native Americans gave a friendly welcome to Christian missionaries. They saw all cultures as being relative, and respected religious freedom. Everyone could choose their beliefs, and change them if they saw fit, without judgment, criticism or hindrance. They resisted the missionaries only when they realised that they were an advance guard of white plunderers, with the backing of a powerful army. Native American philosophy can be summarised as follows: everything which exists finds around it the elements necessary for its existence, the Universe is a form of solidarity and life cannot be imagined in isolation. Everything which exists is influenced by the cycle of ele-

ments, and living creatures are linked together by their breathing, eating, experiences, actions and by the Universe itself. Human beings are not superior beings, nor images of God at the summit of evolution. We must, therefore, live in harmony with nature and not attempt to dominate it. Each thing, living or inanimate, is unique and must be seen as a specific creation of the Universe. Each existence is absolute. Hence Native Americans do not fear death, because they live from the death of plants and animals. What is more, evil does not exist in itself. Justice, like medicine, is there to re-establish trust and as a form of reconciliation with others or with nature. Land does not belong to anyone, not even to a clan or a tribe. When the first Europeans arrived, the Native Americans welcomed them and helped them to set up homes. They only became hostile when the Whites began to behave as if they were dominant, exclusive landlords. For the Native Americans, a tribe is a meeting of individuals and not the sum of the individuals that compose it. When they hold counsel, they try to reach a consensus but pay no attention to any principle of leadership or of majority views. If a consensus cannot be reached, then each person does what they see fit. It was with such people that the great Mason, Albert Pike, lived his years of apprenticeship. This background made him a wonderfully charismatic Mason. When he reached the teaching of the Knight of the Sun, Chief of Masonry, he realised how vital it was and gave it the importance it deserved.

Detail of an engraving depicting the legend of the discovery of one of Hiram's murderers. Eighteenth century.

CHAPTER 15

GREAT BANQUETS

EATING AND DRINKING TOGETHER

THE QUANTITY OF TABLEWARE DECORATED WITH THE ARMS OF LODGES OR MASONIC SYMBOLS, SHOWS HOW IMPORTANT CONVIVIality is for Freemasons.

The banquet is one of the oldest and most solid of Masonic traditions. Anderson's 1723 *Constitutions*, the charter of modern Freemasonry, contains numerous descriptions and references to them. The tradition of the banquet explains the large number of meetings in restaurants and gave rise to the opinion amongst many people in the eighteenth century that Freemasonry was another Bacchic sect, many of which thrived at that time.

In Emulation Working, each meeting is followed by an obligatory banquet, or "fraternal repast". In other rites, this custom is not obligatory. Each year, the French and Scottish Rites have an "Order Banquet". The table is circular, and the Apprentices serve. Lodges also organise solstice festivals which end with a banquet, to which their families and non-Mason friends are sometimes invited.

The ritual of the Order Banquet is taken from the traditions of pre-revolutionary military

lodges in France. In these "works of mastication" or "works of the table", water is called "weak powder", wine "strong powder", champagne "sparkling powder" and spirits "thundering powder". The bread is the "mortar" or "rough ashlar", glasses are "cannons", napkins "flags", forks "picks", knives "swords", food "equipment", the salt "sand" and the pepper "yellow sand". Finally, to fill a glass is "to load". In the eighteenth century, Freemasons met in the banqueting rooms of restaurateurs or innkeepers. They traced symbols on the floor with chalk, then wiped them off after the ceremony and sat down to have dinner. The names of the lodges were often the same as the inns where they met and Freemasons were frequently the butt of jibes because of their banqueting. In 1738, a song about the Freemasons went round Paris: "Let's sing the merit and the glory of Freemasons. Freemasons are fine pretty lads, who meet together just to drink, that's what their hocus pocus is all about."[1]

But, apart from the pleasure it gives us, conviviality also has an important part to play in the history of ideas and customs, and hence of History itself, in the broadest sense of the term.

Glasses engraved with symbols used during banquets or repasts.
They are called "cannons" or "chalices".

The importance of the philosophers' dinners during the Enlightenment is well known. At table, tasty "equipment" washed down with "strong powder" first set tongues wagging, before finally weighing down on the stomach and extinguishing the flames of wit. News is exchanged; stories are told which can be racy or humourous. Witty remarks are sometimes made which go all around town the next day, and disturb the powers that be. Ideas are exchanged and events are discussed. There are surprises, indignation, delight, people moan and people laugh. People who "would otherwise never have met", as the charters of modern Freemasonry put it, philosophers, artists, aristocrats, tradesmen and artisans, often of a modest station, share a meal in a friendly, relaxed atmosphere. Everyone can make their voice heard and everyone is listened to. Let us examine carefully the tableware decorated with the arms of lodges. It honours the banquet, a social event which allows the serious work that was carried out in the workshop, to be continued the following day, to be renewed and give life to the city. The peace, calm and the quality of the work are guaranteed because a time has been set aside for intoxication and regression. For the project to be accomplished, Apollo and Dionysus must take turns in the seat of honour. A repast can also be called an *agape*, a Greek word which means tenderness.

The word tenderness contains notions of affection, love and devotion. The Latin equivalent of agape is *caritas*, which we translate by charity. It is not correct to translate it as love, as in so many contemporary Masonic texts.

Greek opposes *agape* to *eros*. *Eros* is a possessive love, while *agape* is a kind, considerate love. The former is appropriate to the inflamed love of lovers. Over time the meaning evolved until sexual passion became a metaphor for mystical transport and spiritual fervour. This change in meaning is already apparent in Plato's *Phaedrus* and *Symposium*. *Agape* is appropriate to brotherly love, to a calm peaceful love, to love of one's neighbour. The *agape* is thus a sharing of food, of the body, of the heart and of the spirit. And this must be done for pleasure if it is to be profitable. Companions who, as the etymology of the word suggests, share their bread, know that pleasure and happiness are legitimate aims.

1. Translated from *Des fre maçons*, ms. f. 12635, 1738. Bibliothèque nationale de France.

Porcelain made in the Choisy and Creil pottery (France) in 1810.
All of the great European pottery-works produced dinner services for the Masons' tables.

CHAPTER 16

THE MOST COMMON RITES

EXPLORING BEHAVIOUR THROUGH RITUAL

JEAN-MARIE RAGON DE BETTIGNIES (1781–1866), WHO WROTE A NUMBER OF STUDIES OF CEREMONIES AND RITUALS AND EDITED the first French Masonic review, called *Hermès*, drew up a list of fifty-two rites which were practiced by Freemasons. Each involves the progression from one degree (or grade) to another during the course of which symbols are revealed and legendary or historical stories are told. All of them begin with the first three degrees: Apprentice, Fellow and Master.

The word "Scottish" stands for a rite, or rule as they called it in the eighteenth century, which is found all over the world. In 1730, there is a mention in England of a Scottish Masonic grade and, in 1733, there were Scotch Masons' Lodges in London. But it was only on June 25, 1801 that the Ancient and Accepted Scottish Rite was founded in Philadelphia in the USA. It contains thirty-three degrees. Since then, it has spread across the planet. In France, one of this rite's lodges, Les Libres-Penseurs du Pecq, overturned patriarchal thinking in 1882 by admitting a woman, Maria Deraisme. She founded an international body of co-Masonry in 1893, called the Federation of Human Duty, which is still growing in importance in many countries today and which uses the Ancient and Accepted Scottish Rite. France's Grande Loge Féminine, founded in 1952, also works with this rite. Among the exclusively masculine bodies (federations of lodges) in France, the same rite is practiced by the Grande Loge de France, the Grande Loge Nationale Française and by some of the lodges in the Grand Orient de France.

The Rectified Scottish Rite (or rule) was set up between 1778 and 1787 and contains six degrees, while Emulation Working, which rejects the word rite, is the fruit of an 1813 reconciliation between Masons who had been divided since 1753 over that very question of rite and ritual.

Those are the rites which are most commonly practiced throughout the world. But the list would be incomplete if we did not mention the Memphis Rite. It has only a few thousand adepts, but the lodges which practice it can be found on every continent. Its teaching is organised into ninety-five degrees and refers to the Egypt of the Pharaohs. It dates from 1899 with the merger of two rites, Memphis and Mizraïm (Egypt in Hebrew).

The Memphis-Mizraïm Freemasons are not dreamers who spend their lives squeezing drops of sublime truth from hieroglyphics. The best proof

The square and compasses are laid on top of Andersen's Constitutions when used for taking an oath.

CONSTITUTION
DU GRAND ORIENT DE FRANCE

Principes Généraux de l'Ordre Maçonnique

ARTICLE PREMIER

La Franc-Maçonnerie, institution essentiellement philanthropique, philosophique et progressive, a pour objet la recherche de la vérité, l'étude de la morale et la pratique de la solidarité ; elle travaille à l'amélioration de elle et morale, au perfectionnement intellectuel et social de l'humanité.

Elle a pour principes la tolérance mutuelle, le respect des autres et de la liberté absolue de conscience (1).

la discussion de 1876 et du vote de 1877 sur le vœu
premiers termes de 2e paragraphe de l'article premier
si conçus « LA FRANC-MAÇONNERIE A POUR
ALITÉ DE L'AME ».

n'est ni déiste, ni athée, ni même po
solidarité humaine, elle est étrangère
pour principe unique le respect

nous nous livrons en r
ant que le Grand Orien
ortalité de l'âme,
olennellement
ntendons
à not

of this is to note that the first *ad vitam* Grand General Master of the old Memphis Rite (one of the parts composing the present rite) was Giuseppe Garibaldi, the freedom fighter and architect of the Italian republic. He was one of the most remarkable men in history and the fight he led fits well into the Masons' grand project for raising human dignity. The ideals he fought for remain a subject for debate and are still an issue today.

WHAT DO THE MASONIC RITES SAY?

Masonic rituals, organised into specific rites, create an atmosphere which is conducive to the exchange of ideas. One of the characters in brother Goethe's tale *Das Märchen* says: "What shines more brilliantly than gold? Light. What is more dazzling than light? An exchange of ideas."

In the temple, dressed in apron and gloves, everyone listens, watches and participates, in a social group whose aim is to "gather what is scattered and to reach further". This phrase occurs in all the rites and in all commentaries on the rites. It has different levels of meaning: on a social level, it unites persons who would otherwise never have met; on the level of the search for reality, it means advancing into understanding by bringing together different areas of knowledge, by comprehending (from *comprehendere* meaning to grasp).

This is common to all the rites. But each rite also has its own specific traditions and style. The Ancient and Accepted Scottish Rite calls upon the "Great Architect of the Universe", who can be seen as God, or else as a symbol of the

unknowable and of the act of becoming. Its Book of Sacred Law is the Gospel According to Saint John, opened at the first page, which reads: "In the beginning was the Word". In the centre of the lodge, three columns carry candles, which are lit at the start of the work and extinguished at the end. They stand for the trinity of Wisdom-Strength-Beauty. The Rectified Scottish Rite (or rule) also uses Saint John's Gospel and places a broken pillar in the lodge which bears the Latin inscription *adhuc stat* (it is still standing). This rite is unusual in the following way: the fourth symbolic degree, the Scottish Master of Saint Andrew, is complementary to the degree of Master. Emulation Working's distinguishing feature is the way the rituals are recited by heart. What is also exceptional is the fact that offices are rotated. A fixed order determines the officers of the lodges each year. Thus, the Junior Warden becomes the Senior Warden next year, and the Worshipful Master the year after that. The Rite of Memphis focuses more on Egyptian esoteric teaching. One point needs to be clarified. When we use the word "teaching", we do not mean a series of lessons given by a master. The term should be understood in the sense that Aristotle used it when describing how the mysteries of Eleusis conformed to the adage "Do not learn, experience".

All the different lifestyles inspired by the intellectual and spiritual currents of thought that constitute our Græco-Roman, Judæo-Christian civilisation live on in these rites, and are brought to life again and experienced by Freemasons as

A naïve drawing from 1849 depicting a meeting of the Démophiles Lodge, with the names of the participants.

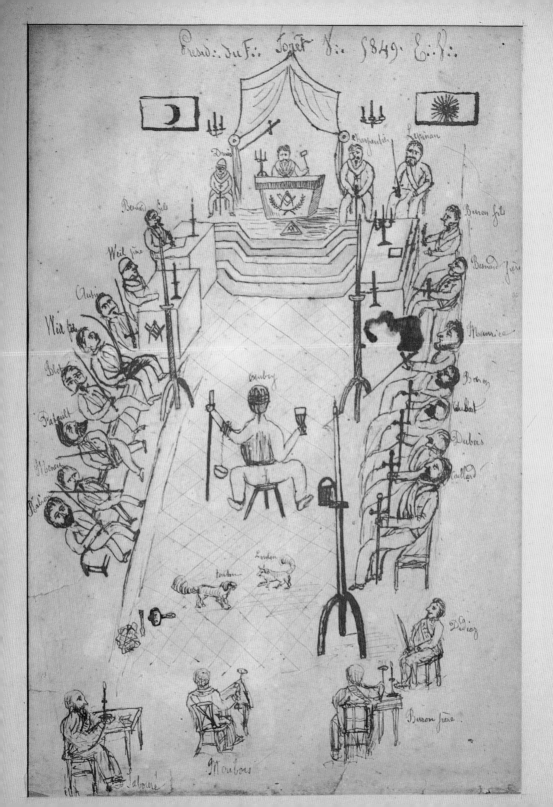

they pass from one grade to the next. There are numerous Old Testament references, particularly in the Ancient and Accepted Scottish Rite. The tradition of chivalry—drawn from the cycle of the Round Table and the adventure of the Templars, including Jacques de Molay's tragic end—lives on, especially in the higher grades of the Scottish rites. Several rites depend on New Testament references, particularly to Saint John's Gospel and the Book of Revelations, as part of the teaching which surrounds the passage from certain grades to others.

Finally, the murder of Hiram, the architect of Solomon's temple, who was killed by three of his fellows, is the central legend of Freemasonry and is taught in all the rites. It is the legend of mastership. At the grade of Master, the Freemason has lived through the passion of Hiram. This legend, which does not figure in the Bible, is extremely ancient and is part of our shared cultural inheritance. It has been made accessible to everyone by Gérard de Nerval in his text *Les nuits du Ramazan*, one of the chapters of his *Voyage en Orient*. And Nerval was not a Freemason.

This brings us to the conclusion of this chapter. Freemasons do not have a special secret, or indeed any secrets. Readers who want to know about the various rites and rituals can turn to books available in shops or libraries throughout the world. Everything has been revealed. But if they memorise the books and try to pass themselves off as Freemasons, then they will quickly be found out, at least by more experienced Masons. Why is this? Just imagine a wine expert who has read everything about wine, but has never tasted any, and who then tries to preach to real connoisseurs.

This takes us back to Aristotle's adage: "Do not learn, experience".

*Detail from a 1745 engraving by Léonard Gabanon depicting
the initiation to the grade of master.*

CHAPTER 17

LODGES OF ADOPTION

BROTHERS AND SISTERS

"ADOPTIVE MASONRY" WAS A FORM OF FEMALE MASONRY PARTICULARLY COMMON IN EIGH-TEENTH-CENTURY FRANCE, BUT WHICH HAS since disappeared. According to the historian Marcy, the oldest known Lodge of Adoption was the Loge de la Félicité in Dieppe, which existed between 1766 and 1773. It was reformed in 1782 and consisted of Masons' wives, daughters, sisters and other close relations. There are traces of four similar lodges in Paris: the Fidélité, the Candeur, the Neufs Sœurs and Saint Jean d'Ecosse du Contrat Social. These lodges were attached to male lodges. The Rite of Adoption had nothing to do with the symbolism of tools and referred above all to the Bible. Its main themes were Eve's apple, Noah's ark and the tower of Babel. There were four degrees in this rite: Apprentice, Fellow, Mistress and perfect Mistress, or perfect Masoness. The Candeur lodge also had a fifth degree of Sublime Scotswoman.

Prior to 1789, the lodges of adoption in France were mostly frequented by aristocratic ladies, such as the Duchesse de Lamballe and the Duchesse de Bourbon. These ladies above all undertook charitable works with great generosity. The Masonry of Adoption survived the Revolution. In 1805, the Empress Josephine

brought it to life again and, on 16 March 1822, the scientist and socialist politician Raspail made a speech at the Lodge of Adoption called the Amis Bienfaisants.

At the beginning of the twentieth century, the Grande Loge de France tried to revive Adoptive Masonry and, from 1901 to 1935, set up ten workshops with this in mind. Then, in 1935, the convent of the Grande Loge de France decided to give the female lodges their indepen-dence and, in 1945, the Union Maçonnique Féminine was founded, which has since become the Grande Loge Féminine de France.

Outside of France there were no female or mixed lodges until the late eighteenth century, although a handful of women have—usually in exceptional circumstances—been accepted into male lodges over the centuries. In the early twentieth century, however, female and "joint" Masonry, linked closely to the French lodges of Adoption and the French tradition, developed in England and the States. Today, the practice of mixed lodges, known as "co-Masonry", continues to develop around the world, though the all-male lodges of the English-speaking world, such as the United Grand Lodge of England, absolutely do not recognise co-Masonic lodges.

Opposite: an eighteenth-century tracing board representing a Lodge of Adoption with the symbols of the higher grades.
Following double page: a nineteenth-century watercolour showing the initiation of a candidate
into a lodge of adoption. The offices of the lodge are being held simultaneously by a man and a woman.

CHAPTER 18

IDEAS AND THE ARTISAN

THOUGHT IS THE RAW MATERIAL

WE HAVE NOW TRACED THE TRADITION IN WHICH MODERN FREEMASONRY EXISTS. THIS TRADITION SERVES AS A MEMORY, WHICH IS vital for creativity, and illustrates the why and wherefore of Freemasonry. There have been Freemasons all over the world since the eighteenth century, but they do not all have the same objectives. They do not all necessarily recognise one another and their different notions of what Freemasonry is, may cause them to reject one another. Sometimes, in the same country even, some are in prison while others are in power!

In terms of religion, there are Masons who are believers and others who are not. The latter may be indifferent to religion, well-disposed to it, or hostile. In politics they may be anarchists, democrats or conservatives, advocates of a free economy or of a planned one, nationalists or internationalists. They represent every current of thought, except for extremists and religious fanatics. If Freemasonry does influence the life of a city, then the city's active life also influences the lodges. The history of Freemasonry is a history of the attempts to annex or manipulate it by every sort of political or religious orthodoxy, by every sort of party that preaches an ideology, and by every sort of pressure group. To understand how Freemasonry works, it is necessary to explore different modes of thought: imagination, reason, intuition, intellectual logic and dream logic all participate in the creation of practical metaphors. The symbolism of tools is basically about the act of becoming. In this context, the intelligence of the brain and the intelligence of the heart feed each other. By the fifteenth century, Marsilio Ficino, who helped establish Florence's Platonic Academy, one of the precursory institutions of modern Freemasonry, had already pointed to the fact that brotherhood, or true friendship, can exist only between those who share a desire to learn, whether it be for pleasure, or to gain a better understanding of the world. The working model for the learned is a logical one, for ideas are the philosopher's raw material. Artisans, on the other hand, transform their raw materials, look after their tools and make new ones, acquire know-how and transmit it. This means there is no dependency or relative order of importance between artisans and philosophers. They are simply analagous and complementary.

Opposite page: a stone-cutter by François Sicard showing the working origins of the Masonic order.
Following double page: a young Mason must learn how to cut stone and is often compared to unhewn rock. Cut stone stands for a Mason's evolution. Masons are described as adding their cut stone to the edifice of humanity.

CHAPTER 19

BECOMING
A FREEMASON

REACHING FURTHER

PEOPLE GENERALLY BECOME FREEMASONS BY RECOMMENDATION. ALL CANDIDATES HAVE A SPONSOR. WHEN A LODGE HAS BEEN informed that it has a new candidate, it votes to see if it will consider accepting them. The Worshipful Master then appoints three investigators, who work in ignorance of one another. Each investigator meets the candidate and drafts a report which is read out in the lodge. Then the candidate's photo, with name, address and profession are put up on a noticeboard in a place frequented by all the members of the obedience, so that brethren from other lodges can examine them. After that, the blindfolded candidate must undergo questioning. They are received in the lodge with their eyes blindfolded and are questioned by the brethren who have already listened to the investigators' reports. Finally, after this questioning, they vote to admit or reject the candidate. A simple majority is not enough, however. Some lodges insist on a unanimous election, while most demand at least three-quarters majority. This procedure is not followed everywhere. Some lodges receive their candidates in the antechamber of the temple, or in an adjacent office, and do not question them. In this case, the investigators have a greater responsibility.

FAMOUS FREEMASONS
The following list is not exhaustive. Its purpose is to show how varied the different ways of thinking are in lodges.

A large number of Napoleon's Marshals and members of the Bonaparte family, but not Napoleon himself (despite a long-standing rumour to the contrary); many anarchists, such as Joseph Proudhon, Bakunin, Kropotkin and Francisco Ferrer; freedom fighters such as Simon Bolivar, San Martin, Benito Juarez, Giuseppe Garibaldi, La Fayette, Rochambeau, Benjamin Franklin and Washington; various kings, princes and royalists, the Duke of Brunswick (who was a Grand Master), certain kings of England (Edward VII, George VI), Frederick the Great, who was also a musician and the author of an important Masonic text, the *Anti-Machiavel*, some kings of Sweden, Duke Decaze the Prime Minister of Louis XVIII, Prince Murat, who was also a Grand Master under the reign of Napoleon III, and Emir Abd el-Kader. Among the leaders of modern democracies it will be sufficient to mention no less than fourteen American Presidents, including Theodore Roosevelt, Harry Truman and Gerald Ford, and high-ranking politicians and ministers such as Jules Ferry, Winston Churchill

Detail of a bronze statue depicting Voltaire (1694–1778),
initiate in the Neufs Sœurs Lodge.

and Cecil J. Rhodes. We should also mention here one of the most eminent Freemasons of this century, Tomás Garrigue Masaryk (1886–1948), the founder of the Republic of Czechoslovakia. This remarkable man also wrote a number of richly varied influential books, such as *On Suicide, Pascal, The Foundations of Concrete Logic, The Social Question* (1898) which is an analysis and refutation of Marxism, and *Modern Man and Religion* (1934) which argues for freedom of religious belief. He also wrote several fascinating studies on the work of Goethe, Byron, Musset, Zola, Maupassant, Shelley, Poe and Baudelaire.

Many writers, artists and intellectuals can also be cited: Helvetius, Voltaire, Montesquieu, Condorcet, Lessing, Goethe, Herder, Wieland, Pushkin, Carducci, Kipling, Mark Twain, Sir Walter Scott, Oscar Wilde, Robert Burns, Mozart, Haydn and Glück. Not forgetting such varied characters as Davy Crockett, Duke Ellington, Louis Armstrong, Pierre Dac, Houdini and Kurt Tucholski.

Hungary owes its freedom to a remarkable Freemason, Lajos Kossuth (1802–1894). During Kossuth's lifetime, nationalist feelings were closely linked with fundamental values such as human rights, justice and individual liberty. Kossuth's nationalism, like that of other Freemasons such as Garibaldi, Bolivar or San Martin, entailed a defence of freedom and a rejection of feudal society. Finally, in Russia there were a number of Freemasons in Kerenski's government prior to the Revolution, first and foremost Kerenski himself.

Opposite: Wolfgang Amadeus Mozart at a Masonic meeting, in a detail from a painting (overleaf) showing Mozart in the Espérance Nouvellement Couronnée Lodge, around 1790. Historisches Museum der Stadt Wien.

CONCLUSION

The legends told in Masonic rites mix historical facts with written and oral traditions of often obscure origins, with a view to giving memories and actions a field of reference. Rituals create meaning which, as it gradually solidifies, forms first a backbone then a solid set of foundations. The community of Freemasons, which visits these strange landscapes, tests itself by means of these marvellous tales of a real and imagined past. How and why do contemporary human beings, haunted by the desire to master their destiny, turn to such Masonic folklore? It is partly because Freemasonry's varied rituals allow the voices of past generations to be heard above the chatter of fashionable current ideas. All over the world, we lay aside our layman's rags and allow historical and legendary characters to dress us in clothes of light. To reach further is, after all, to gather together. The ancient symbol of the circle, with its radii meeting in the centre, symbolises this idea.

Traditionalists are united against this approach. They want to be witnesses of the beginning, guardians of permanence, or militants for a return. If we truly want to "reach further" then we may consider them as carriers of flames, but not bearers of the Light. The old opposition between conservatives and progressionists, mystics and the enlightened, or spiritualists and materialists has now been surpassed. But, we have to be careful! The approach taken here should never be raised to the level of absolute truth, nor such a truth turned into an orthodoxy! Our own dialogue is enlightening. That is its aim, but it does not enlighten everything. To do that, it must necessarily be linked to all the other various and opposed approaches that exist.

The new pattern of thinking recognises the divisions in nature as being a functional necessity and a historical fact. At the same time it waits for them to multiply and be obliterated. Hermes, the god who sets limits, also teaches us how to cross them. The myth of Hermes shows us how boundaries (*hermeion*) are there to be crossed. Thus, as a young smiling god-child, he cheekily steals a number of his brother Apollo's herd to give to mankind. Now men and gods have to negotiate and reach an agreement if they want their herds of cattle to multiply. ... And the theft is pardoned because it made Zeus laugh. Hermes both guides travellers and leads them astray. The three brothers—Apollo, Dionysus and Hermes—who are often opposed and always complementary, are the princes of the Kingdom of the Mothers, which it is up to us to explore, using the builder's tools: the square, compasses, lever, chisel, gauge and all the other instruments of measurement.

An eighteenth-century tracing board showing the fourteenth degree of the Ancient and Accepted Scottish Rite.

GLOSSARY

Like every craft, Freemasonry has its jargon. It uses familiar words but gives them a special meaning, suited to its art and customs. Symbols are universal, but Freemasons link them, organise them and comment on them in their own particular way. Discussions of symbols often contain terms whose meanings also need to be explained. This glossary explains some commonly used terms and provides information which will come in useful when reading or listening to discussions on the subject of Freemasonry.

APRON: an essential item of Masonic dress, consisting of a rectangle and a triangular bib. An Apprentice's apron is white. A Fellow's is sometimes white with blue edging. At the degree of Master and beyond, the colour and ornamentation of the apron varies. Aprons are generally lined in black, with silver stripes.

FREEMASON: the etymology of this term has long been disputed. There are three possibilities to choose from:
- *Free-stone Mason*: a term applied to a Mason who sculpted soft stone; as opposed to a *Rough-stone Mason* who worked on hard stone. With his gavel and chisel, a soft-stone Mason could sculpt more elaborate figures in high or low relief.
- "Free" meaning the opposite of enslaved. According to feudal law people belonged to the overlord of a particular area. Emancipation

exempted them from certain obligations towards their lord, such as the duty to stay in one place and serve him. "Free" masons, therefore had the right to travel and work wherever they chose.
- "Free" being the status of the trade, rather than the person, Masonry being a *francmestier* or "emancipated trade". According to Etienne Boileau's admirable *Livre des métiers* (1268), stone-cutters were given their freedom, but not masons, carpenters or plasterers.

GRAND LODGE: In Great Britain this term describes a federation of lodges which observe the same rite or the supreme governing body of the Masons.

GRAND ORIENT: In France and Europe generally, this term is used for a federation of lodges.

GRAND EAST: In the United States, the place where the Grand Lodge meets, thus the seat of Masonic authority.

INITIATION: ceremony which consecrates the admission of a candidate into a lodge. Masonic initiation has kept some of the characteristics of the initiation into the trade which it originated from. In general terms, the initiation rite is a rite of passage.

LODGE: the lodge is the physical place where Freemasons meet. This may be a building or location which is specially set aside and

arranged for Masonic meetings, but not necessarily so. Originally, working Masons would have had a lodge on every building site to keep their tools in and to meet for meals with their colleagues.
Seven Freemasons can "hold a lodge meeting" wherever they wish, at someone's house, in an inn, or in the open air. During the war, Freemasons founded lodges in the concentration camps and initiated new members there.
The "lodge" is also the term used for a group of Freemasons who work together under a "distinctive title" or group name, for example Mozart's lodge was called *A la Bienfaisance* (loosely translated as the Lodge of Good Works), and Jules Ferry's was *La Clémente Amitié* (Merciful Friendship).

MEETING: a Masonic assembly. Masons are described as "holding lodge meetings".

OFFICES AND OFFICERS: these are the posts within a lodge and the brethren who fill them: the Worshipful Masters preside over the lodge with their teams, the College of Officers. The Senior Wardens are in charge of the south pillar, where the Fellows sit, and the Junior Wardens are in charge of the north pillar, where the Apprentices sit. The Secretaries are the lodges' memory: taking minutes at meetings, keeping the archives and looking after any correspondence. The Orators make sure that the law and rules are respected. It is the Orators who decide whether a vote would be appropriate and, when necessary, give their opinions concerning a debate. They can contest the Worshipful Master if they think that officer has made a mistake. In addition, they give the speech of welcome to new initiates. The Hospitalers, or Almoners, collect and manage the charity fund. The Treasurers look after the lodges' finances. They collect subscriptions and approve expenditure. The Deacons and the Masters of Ceremonies ensure that the rituals and ceremonies are correctly observed. The Tylers or Inner Guards watch the entrance and make certain that the "lodge is duly tiled" before work begins, ensuring that no member of the lodge or visitor from another lodge is still waiting outside in the antechamber.

ORDER or CRAFT: these terms stand for the brotherhood of Masonry in general, the Masonic Order is also known as The Craft. Some Grand Lodges, however, have adopted the term order for themselves, but only when they have an international jurisdiction, for example the Co-Masonic Federation of Human Duty and the Order of Memphis.
The term "craft" was the corporate term used by the medieval guilds and is current in England. In France, the term "order" is more usual: it has been carried over from religious orders and royal preferments such as the Order of the Holy Ghost.

ORIENT: light, and therefore power, comes from the East, where the sun rises. Most civilizations of the northern hemishpere have revered the East as the most important point on the compass. The Orient is the part of the lodge where the Worshipful Master sits.

RITE: the etymology of this term leads us to think of arrangement, succession, of number and of order (Greek *arithmos*, number; Sanskrit *rtam* order or conformity). A rite is a set of ceremonies observed in a certain order. By extension, a rite is also a moment in a ceremony, for example the rite of entering the lodge, the rite of establishing the officers, and so on. A Masonic rite consists of a set of rituals made up of a varying number of degrees (or grades) of advancement, the first three of which are always Apprentice, Fellow and Master. The Ancient and Accepted Scottish Rite includes thirty-three degrees, the French Rite seven, and the Memphis Rite ninety-five. Emulation Working uses only the first three grades and prefers the term Working to Rite. The Rectified Scottish System (synonymous with Rite) appeared in France in 1778 and rejected the term Rite, replacing it with *Régime*.
Rites vary according to their style and their teachings. The most commonly observed rites in Europe are the Ancient and Accepted Scottish Rite, the French Rite, the Rectified Scottish Rite, Emulation Working and the Memphis Rite. A Grand

Lodge or Grand Orient can bring together lodges which observe different rites.

TEMPLE: this word has several meanings in Freemasonry:
- the place where the lodge meets;
- the temple of Jerusalem;
- a sacred place. This is the original Latin meaning of the word.

WARDEN: see OFFICES AND OFFICERS.

WORKSHOP: term given to any organisation of Freemasons. There are no lone Freemasons. According to the degrees (or grades), workshops have different names. In the first three grades, which are used in all the rites (see above), it is a lodge (see above). At higher grades, there are numerous other terms: lodge of perfection, chapter, council, archilodge, college, Areopagus, consistory, encampment, supreme council. Other names also exist, such as court, Court of Sinai, hierarchy or Third Heaven. Each term is linked to a particular ritual. The workshop is arranged according to the ritual being enacted, and the brethren wear the appropriate aprons, sashes and collars.

BIBLIOGRAPHY

J. ANDERSEN, The Constitutions of the Free-Masons, (facsimile edition). Quatuor Coronati Lodge, London, 1976.

D. BÉRESNIAK, Les Premiers Médicis et l'Académie platonicienne de Florence. Détrad, Paris, 1985.

D. BÉRESNIAK, Rites et Symboles de la franc-maçonnerie, tI "Loges bleues", tII "Hauts Grades". Détrad, Paris, 1994.

D. BÉRESNIAK, La Franc-Maçonnerie. J. Grancher, Paris, 1988.

J. FONTAINE, L'Éveil, de l'initiation au maître. Détrad, Paris, 1995

A. HORNE, King Solomon's Temple in the Masonic Tradition. HarperCollins, New York, 1989.

B. JONES, Freemason's Guide and Compendium. Harrap, London, 1950.

W. KIRK MACNULTY, Freemasonry. A Journey through Ritual and Symbol. Thames and Hudson, London, 1991.

D. KNOOP, The Genesis of Freemasonry. Manchester University Press, 1949.

D. LIGOU, Dictionnaire universel de la franc-maçonnerie. PUF, Paris, 1974.

A. G. MACKEY, The History of Freemasonry. Gramercy Books, New York, 1996.

A. POZARNIK, Mystères et Actions du rituel d'ouverture en loge maçonnique. Dervy, Paris, 1993.

J. TRESCASES, L'Etoile flamboyante. Trédaniel, Paris, 1989.

A. E. WAITE, A New encyclopedia of Freemasonry. Wings Books, New York, 1996.

O. WIRTH, La Franc-Maçonnerie rendue intelligible à ses adeptes, t I "l'apprenti", t II "le compagnon", t III "le maître". Dervy, Paris, 1945.

PHOTOGRAPHIC CREDITS

All photographs © Laziz Hamani/Editions Assouline. The photographs were taken on the occasion of the exhibition Franc-Maçonnerie, Avenir d'une tradition, Musée des Beaux-Arts de Tours, 1997. The editor would like to thank the following institutions for giving permission to photograph objects on loan from their collections: Loge de la Parfaite Union, Mons (p. 13, 27, 105, 119); Musée de la Loge Les Démophiles, Tours (pp. 33, 48–49, 51, 70–1, 85, 101, 123); Musée des Beaux-Arts de Tours (pp. 53, 55, 109); Musée de la Grande Loge de France, Paris (front cover, endpapers, pp. 38–9, 44, 46, 59, 62, 67, 69, 78, 86–7, 89, 93, 94, 96, 103, 106–7, 110–1, 113, 126–7, back cover); Musée du Grand Orient de France, Paris (p. 63, 83); Collection Détrad-Avs, Paris (p. 65); Prins Frederik Museum, The Hague (pp. 66, 124–5); Historisches Museum der Stadt Wien (pp. 115–7).

Opposite: carved rough ashlar from the Démophiles Lodge. Nineteenth century.
Following double page: diorama showing the role of the arts and sciences in a lodge. Eighteenth century.
Pages126–127: initiation to the grade of apprentice. Engraving by Gabanon, 1745.

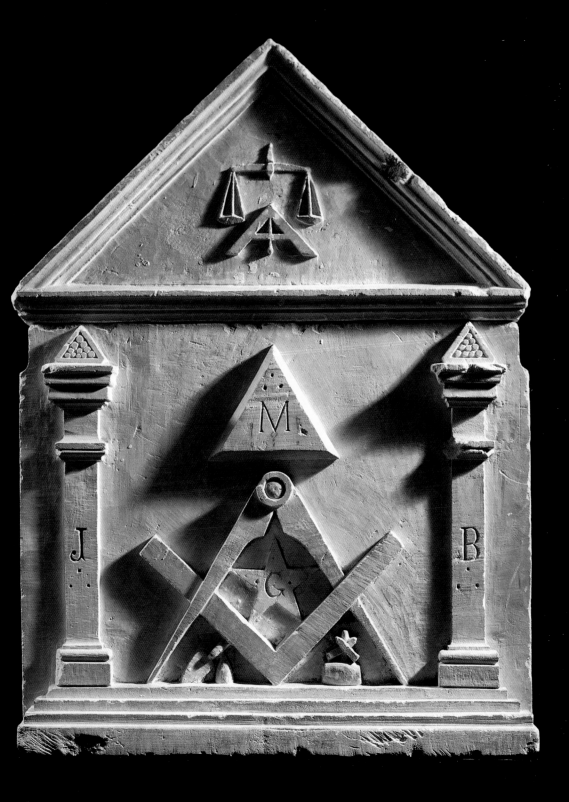

1. Le Grand Maître.
2. le p.ʳ Surveillant.
3. le 2.ᵉ Surveillant.
4. le Recipiendaire.

Assemblée de Francs-Maçon.
Entrée du Rec
Dedié au très Galant, très sincere et très veridique Frere
Dessiné par Madame la Marqu

la Reception des Apprentifs.
e dans la Loge.
onard Gabanon, Auteur du Catechisme des Francs-Macons.
t Gravé par Mademoiselle ✳✳✳✳.

5. l'Orateur.
6. le Secretaire
7. le Tresorier
8. le Frere Sentinelle

ACKNOWLEDGMENTS

First of all I wish to thank Claudine, my wife. Ever-attentive to my well-being, she has created a home atmosphere conducive to my work. What is more, she is the first to read what I have written and her criticism is often helpful. My thanks also go to my son, Ariel, who despite his busy life has been teaching Claudine and me how to use a computer.

This book could never have been assembled were it not for the help of certain friends, who gave us access to rare documents, allowed us to photograph objects and helped us in our choices. Jean-Philippe Marcovici, president of the 5997 Association, who organised the Freemasonry exhibition at Tours (1997), allowed us to photograph rare items from European collections which we would never have gained access to without his kind assistance. What is more, Jean-Philippe opened the doors to us of the lodge where the Démophiles meet. This temple, where I had the honour of taking the floor, is a vital part of our country's contemporary history and one of the most beautiful buildings ever consecrated to the work of the Freemasons. Thank you, Jean-Philippe. Philippe Morbach is the Keeper of the Museum of the Grande Loge de France. His expertise and erudition are recognised and appreciated throughout Europe. To these qualities must be added his kindness and generosity. We are indebted to him for letting us see many extremely beautiful and interesting documents and objects and helping us make a selection. All our gratitude to him. At the Grande Loge de France, we should also like to thank Maurice Bonnefoy, the archivist, Jonathan Giné and François Rognon, the librarian, for their invaluable help. Paul Gordot is the Keeper of the Museum of the Grand Orient de France. He trusted us with the treasures he so carefully conserves and beautifully displays for the museum's many visitors. My thanks to him. My thanks go also to Daniel Ribes, who entrusted aprons and other items he had made to Laziz Hamani. As director of the Editions Détrad-Avs and maker of Masonic regalia, Daniel is always helpful in his efforts to aid researchers and creators. Laziz Hamani, who took the photographs published in this book, is my co-author because the text and images reflect each other. Our work together was an enjoyable experience. What words can express his artistry? His skill and love of beauty create a nobility of colour which is an honour to us all. My thanks to him for this. Finally, my gratitude to Marc-Alain Ouaknin, for introducing me to Martine and Prosper Assouline, the publishers of this remarkable series of books.

Laziz Hamani would like to thank Jonathan Kluger for his invaluable help in producing these images, and Philippe Sébirot for the direction which he gave to this book. Thanks to Daniel Delisle of the Studio Prumelle, to Paulette and Jean-Pierre Rolland of Tours and to Daniel Béresniak for his incomparable way of explaining things with simplicity and warmth.

Finally, the editor would like to thank Peter Bloch for his kind assistance in providing documentation for this English adaptation of the original French publication, and John Hamill of the United Grand Lodge, London, for his invaluable advice and for so generously sparing his time to read through the English manuscript.